Lif
Without
Coffee

Donated to Binley woods
Primary School PTA.

June 2019

Dr Afiniki Akanet

AGE

Life Without Coffee
by Afiniki Akanet

© Afiniki Akanet 2017

Produced and published in 2017
by Affinity Global Enterprises (AGE) Ltd
www.afiniki.co.uk

A catalogue card for this book is available from the British Library
Paperback ISBN: 978-0-9573247-3-2
Ebook ISBN: 978-0-9573247-4-9

Publication managed by TJ INK
www.tjink.co.uk

Printed and bound in Great Britain by TJ International

For my dear children,
Sophie and David.

Appreciation

I am very grateful to my loving husband, family and friends who always encourage and support me. Special thanks to my publishers and readers who make writing worthwhile.

Introduction

"I don't know how you manage without coffee" is a comment I usually get when I tell people that I do not drink coffee. They sometimes even make it sound like I am 'abnormal' for not drinking or liking coffee. At times, I wonder if I am truly missing out on something great by not drinking coffee. Even my own husband has told me about the energy boost he gets from drinking coffee, and it makes me wonder if I could do so much better with coffee.

On the other hand, I think of how many times coffee lovers have said, "Wait till you ...., then you will have to start drinking coffee". The comments have included "Wait till you start medical school", "Wait till your final exams", "Wait till you start work", "Wait till you do those night shifts", "Wait till you have postgraduate exams" and "Wait till you have children", but as you can probably tell, I am now a wife, mother and medical doctor (among other things) who does not drink coffee. This is not because it is a sin to drink coffee, but because I personally do not like it and have developed other ways to keep stimulated and motivated.

I have seen funny posters that say "A life without coffee is no life" or "A life without coffee is scary". I imagine this is probably true for a real caffeine addict, but I have to say that I have just never been interested in drinking coffee or other stimulants/energy drinks. I am also not judging those who love coffee or energy drinks, but I do believe that too much of anything is not good. As we say in the medical world, **the difference between a drug and a poison is the dose**.

Although this book is starting off with coffee-drinking, it is really an opportunity for me to share what I call my coffee-substitute. If you like your tea or coffee, this book can give you more of a driving force and pointers to a less stressful life. If you are a hot-chocolate-girl like me, I hope that this book adds a buzz to your sweetness and gives you a drive for more intentional living. In short, this is my attempt to answer the recurring question "How do you do it?".

Chapter 1

Don't we all just love those days when we wake up with a plan and go to bed feeling that it has all gone well? For me, the best days are the ones that start calmly with quiet time in the morning, getting ready without feeling rushed, arriving where I want to go on time, getting things done as planned and coming home before my family to get things ready for a nice wind-down and dinner at the table. I find this sets the tone for the rest of the evening, because a nice 'dinner and download', as I call it, helps everyone feel more able to relax and do whatever else needs doing that evening so that we can get to bed at a decent time, ready for the next day. This may sound like 'Miss Perfect' to some people, but it is possible to have this most days if you really want to. I think Mr/Miss Perfect is the person that manages this kind of day, everyday! If there is no outing planned for your day – if you are off work or a stay-at-home parent, for example – it is good to have a plan for the day anyway, so that even relaxation time is intentional and the day does not just pass by with no purpose.

I am not saying that I have it all together, but I try to live a fruitful and enjoyable life. This is not about trying to be perfect, but about being able to reflect and improve daily. I personally find it helpful to be able to 'download' at the end of the day. The workplace can sometimes become so tense, competitive and fast-paced, that people just have to keep going even when there are conversations that need to be had. Sometimes, we choose not to say what needs to be said at work or college, for fear of being judged, misunderstood or misquoted. This is really sad, especially when you consider that many people spend most of their waking hours with their colleagues. Even staying at home with children can leave you feeling drained when you have to pick your battles and be careful what you say to them. It is nice to have someone to share your deep thoughts with.

Even if you live alone, a phone conversation to discuss your day and get things off your chest can help reduce stress building up and gets you more prepared for the next day. I laughed when I heard somewhere years ago that "A spouse is someone who is there to witness your life". It is nice to have someone, anyone, to share your sadness, achievements, laughter, concerns and silly thoughts with. As much as we like minding our own business, we are also social beings, so it is worth making an effort to build and maintain good relationships with others. I know that this does not come naturally to everyone, but experience has taught me that staying connected is good for mental wellbeing.

It is good to have someone who really knows you. It may be a parent, sibling, friend, spouse, co-worker or professional, and it takes time and energy to build this kind of relationship. Both parties also need to value the relationship so that it can work. You cannot know someone much better than knowing what they do, feel and say everyday. This is why I find the 'download' useful for strengthening relationships and maintaining the feeling of being valued and understood.

For children, it helps their self-esteem to feel that adults care enough to hear their thoughts and try to understand their feelings. Even if you do not have someone to listen to your own problems, be that someone for a child. Not everyone likes to talk, and some people might find it sufficient to talk properly with a friend or spouse once a week, once a month, or when it is absolutely necessary. It is important to know what works for you so that you are not building up pressure inside and breaking down every few months or years!

Talking regularly with my mother when I was younger really helped me to analyse my feelings about issues and to reassess the direction of my life from time to time. For some, it may be an aunt, uncle or friend that gives them that listening ear. Sadly, it becomes hard work when you try to 'download' in detail to more than one person everyday, so as I grew older, I spoke more to my boyfriend (who later became my husband) and less to my mother, who understands and still has a good relationship with me. I think this is one of the reasons why it is hard to have an affair without getting caught! It is almost like serving two masters when you try to have that level of intimacy with more than one person, but I am sure that there are some good pretenders and cheating spouses who manage it well out there. It does defeat the purpose, however, when such deep conversations become a game of lies rather than a heart connection.

At this juncture, I would also like to emphasise how important it is for parents to remember the fact that children will not remain children forever. I, personally, will feel that I have done a great job as a mother when my children are able to live fulfilled, happy lives, with or without me. Some parents cling tightly to or control their adult children for selfish reasons, not realising that a parent-child relationship was not designed to satisfy the need for companionship. It should be about care not control. Children should be allowed to grow and see the world for themselves. A good, responsible person will still care for their parents even after gaining independence. If we are aware of the fact that children will want their own lives in future, we will not put a complete stop to ours for their sakes. Loving your children is different from smothering them, or using them as an excuse not to do anything with your own life. We must stop dreaming of the good old days when they were babies and look forward to the great years ahead when they can make their own good decisions and raise their own happy families. This is our time to influence the children's future – let us make the most of it and remain a good example to them always. I am glad my parents did that for me, and you can learn to do same for children, whatever happened in your own childhood.

Back to the issue of sharing our lives – I noticed as I grew older that I had more than one 'best friend', each with his/her 'specialist' area. It is a privilege to have many friends, and I believe **it is wisdom to choose who you discuss what with**. Some people will have a friend they talk with for money issues, one for work matters, one for relationship issues etc. The friend will usually be chosen for this subject area because of their life experience and/or our experiences with them. It is important to remember though that **friendship is not about gaining approval; it is about being honest, open and accepted.** Understanding this fact can reduce a lot of stress for some people who constantly keep up appearances to impress 'friends'.

It is fantastic if you have *one* great friend who you feel can understand you in *every* area of life. Those are what teenage girls call their BFFs, I think. Unfortunately, not everyone has a Best Friend Forever (BFF). Some friendships are only for a season of your life and there is nothing wrong with that, because people grow and change. Some friends will grow together and accept the changes in each other, while others will have to drift apart as they change and move on in life. An old African proverb translates as "Twenty children cannot play together for twenty years". You can have a more peaceful life by recognising when relationships have come to a significant junction or even to their natural end. It does not necessarily mean that you or they are bad – it is sometimes just the end of an era, which opens doors for new things, if we let it.

If you are the friend who people like to open up to, you need to be careful to have your own carefully chosen outflow channels too. This can be especially relevant for people in mentoring and leadership positions. I can tell you from experience that it can become draining hearing all about other people's problems and having little opportunity to talk about yours. That is why most caring professions encourage debriefs, supervision, mentoring, pastoral support and activities outside work.

In a traditional home, the woman is usually 'the one to talk to'. A wife and mother usually wants to emotionally support her husband and children whenever needed. In some families, the father has to be the 'emotional rock' for the children, due to the mother's illness, absence, personality etc. The first step in managing stress that might arise from this is to recognise that you have this important role. You must then decide how best you can manage it without damaging your own physical and mental health. Identify your stress triggers and know the warning signs, so you can be there for your friends and family for longer. This will involve being 'selfish' at times and taking a break. Whether it is time alone, an evening out with friends, a weekend away with your partner, or a day with your own parent or best friend (without the children), you will feel refreshed and more effective afterwards.

Another way of managing this will be to actively choose who you allow to 'download' on you. As a wife and mother, my husband and children get priority over anyone else. If listening to certain people drains you so much so that you do not have any emotional energy left for your family, it may be useful to reduce the amount of time you spend talking with them. Most of the time, we burden ourselves with issues that will be resolved with or without our help. **People who always take without giving will soon find someone else to take from, if you step back!**

As a woman who has a lot on her plate, I realised that certain conversations are not very useful, so I have cut down on those to make time for more productive things in my life. I also take time to regularly assess what is 'on my plate' so that I am not unintentionally drawn into a 'busy' and unhappy lifestyle. I have noticed that people sometimes love to be 'busy' – taking on more than they can handle and having no time for rest and relaxation. We somehow feel that being busy makes us look more important. I personally think it is more respectable to be approachable, productive and efficient. If that leads to being busy at times, then that is okay, but I do not think that being 'too busy' should be our regular status. Although, for some unhelpful activities and issues, I will always be 'too busy' – it is all about priorities!

When you hear the word 'priorities', what do you think about? What is most important to you in your life? It is obviously different for everyone. Priorities also vary at different stages of life. There was a time in my life when studying to become a medical doctor was the priority. I knew from childhood that medicine is what I wanted to do. I would give up anything that tried to get in the way of my achieving that dream. I remember I was such a 'one-way street' about it that I even gave up *free* piano lessons because I needed to prepare for important exams. Now as a doctor, I admire musicians so much and sometimes wish I made more effort to learn music as well. There is much to admire in people who learn to balance many aspects of life successfully from an early age. On the other hand, I have also met doctors who are great musicians but think that writing a book is something they could never do.

We all have different talents. No one has it all, but we can each make the best of what we have. Now, with more commitments, it has become harder for me to make time for piano lessons, but I believe it must not be a real passion for me or else I would have done it! This is where knowing your forte comes in. I am ashamed to say that I never did well with music even in school, so pursuing the dream of becoming a great pianist will be a very uphill journey for me, because it is not one of my talents. I enjoy good music and sometimes wish I was talented in that area, but I would rather work on what I am naturally talented at, so that I can make the best of my time on earth. This does not mean never learning anything difficult. I am referring to the idea of choosing your battles. When you have a focus, it is easier to decide which challenges are worth taking on. 'Knowing my forte' is not an excuse for not doing things I do not like. I have had to learn subjects and skills I do not naturally enjoy, or excel at, in order to get to where I am today.

It is important to try something wholeheartedly before concluding that you are not good at it, if it is something you really want to do. I have met lazy people who stay stuck in life, just based on the assumption that they cannot do better. Yes, I think it is laziness not to try, and I am sometimes guilty of it myself. At the end of one's life, the real regrets are the things we could have done but never did, not the things that did not work out after we tried our best. I once had a serious car accident, which I miraculously survived. For me, the thought of death was not as scary as it should have been, because I felt I was living a fruitful life. I could be sad about what I may never have achieved if I had been killed, but I chose to focus on and be pleased about what I have tried and even achieved already in my lifetime. I feel I was kept alive for a reason and that makes me value my time so much more. Although driving is something I have never liked doing, I do what I have to do (when my husband is not free to come along and drive!) and appreciate the blessing of having a car.

Passivity and stagnancy is no way to live. I agree that some days and weeks may be slower than others. I also have days and even months where I am just barely functioning in one area or another, for various reasons. The main thing is to keep pressing on, even when you do not feel like it. If we keep moving forward and doing our best, we will achieve more than we ever imagined. There will definitely be tough times, but every 'failure' has a lesson and matures us with experience. If we do not try, we will never know. Trying allows us to begin to understand how we really feel about our dreams, what the task actually involves and whether we really want to carry on.

On the other hand, there are those who will "try anything once". When people say that, I laugh and say silently, **"Be careful – 'once' could be too much"**. Apart from the obviously dangerous things, a principled person will not try '*anything* once'. If something does not fit in with my beliefs and life goals, it could be dangerous to try it even once. There are people who are sadly still paying for the folly of their youth in ways they never imagined. The aspiring politician who tried something stupid once in his past will tell you how much better his career could be without that scandal!

I feel that knowing what I want out of life, my aims for each day and my goals for each year helps me to stay focussed so that I am not wasting energy on unproductive things and distractions. Having a focus also helps me to manage my time, making allowance for sleep and play. Yes, play! Even when I had the scariest exams and meetings to prepare for, I kept stress under control by allowing time for 'play'.

Play, for me, has been activities like watching comedy, exercising, shopping, listening to music and spending time with my family. I find that taking a couple of hours out to relax helps me to be more productive with the working hours I have left. As much as I like being productive with my time and money, I truly believe that sometimes you just need to relax and enjoy the moments. For example, I would gladly rearrange my deadlines, where possible, to take a day off to recharge when tired, so that I am not requiring coffee to stay awake and meet that initial target. An intentional break is very different from laziness and procrastination. That short break might be the difference between falling ill and a good finish.

I will not deny that there are several times in my life when I have had to survive on little sleep (still with no coffee), but I believe the time spent unwinding helped my sleep to be more refreshing and my waking hours to be more productive. This only works, of course, if it is planned in advance. I cannot imagine a student, who has done no studying all year, to be able to take out time to relax when he has so much to revise in two days! Or a woman expecting guests for dinner in two hours being able to sit and watch a movie when she has not even bought or prepared any of the food. Unless, maybe, they do not mind failing the exam, asking guests to bring their own food or cancelling the dinner last minute!

Life is all about choices. This is why I choose the path of least unnecessary stress. **Less stress does not mean less work.** It is possible for someone who works very hard to be less stressed than someone who watches television all day dreading the bills at the end of the month! I realise, though, that stress means different things to different people. Some people enjoy the last minute rush, while people like me prefer the forward planning. The problem only arises when 'last minute people' try to stress me out with their avoidable problems because I look calm after I have done my work/preparation in advance! This is when the polite 'No' comes in handy, unless of course I am actually available to help.

I have always believed that anyone can have it all. You cannot *do* it all, but you can have it all, when you set sensible goals and have a good attitude. It is difficult to judge when you have arrived at your destination if you did not have one from the beginning. The destination is your big life goal or focus, while the goals are the daily, monthly or yearly targets that must fit in with your destination or purpose. I often sit with my husband and discuss where we are on the contentment scale. It usually ends up as a session of counting our blessings because we like to be thankful in every circumstance. We know that life is full of ups and downs, but it is possible to be contented when you acknowledge your achievements (no matter how small) and recognise that the disappointments are only challenges to be overcome.

Being thankful and aware of your achievements fuels the motivation to carry on. Sometimes it is hard to see the achievements when there are large disappointments or huddles in your way. An attitude of gratitude helps one to appreciate even the very life, health and sanity we use to talk about our problems. No matter how bad a situation is, there is always something to be grateful for because it really could be worse. This attitude has helped me through many difficult times and given me the energy to hope and press on. **Seeing your problems from a winning perspective helps you to think of solutions** or have the strength to wait it out, for those problems that you can really do nothing about.

People sometimes avoid having goals in order to avoid disappointment. I think disappointment is a part of life. If you have lived long enough, you would have faced some big ones. Dealing with disappointments in a healthy way is better than avoiding them. Someone who wishes to be married, for example, could feel that this is something they cannot force and should not bother setting goals about. I know how hard it can be to meet people these days and I agree that love cannot be forced, but there is no harm in setting goals to do with socialising or meeting people, as this fits in with the aim of finding a life partner. A single man or woman could look at a new friendship as an achievement towards their goal of getting married one day to that person or someone else, because both good and bad experiences with people tell us more about ourselves and prepare us for the future. Any new friend is an addition to your network of contacts. You never know who you might meet through whom!

A way of reducing the possibility of disappointments that may arise from friendships could be to take time to know people's expectations and values before getting into an intimate relationship or courtship with them, saving the most valued aspects of yourself for the one you choose to marry, focusing on improving your own life in the meantime, and finding a way to feel whole and happy in yourself so that you are not desperate for someone to complete you. It is a shame when intelligent and beautiful people get so desperate and worried about their increasing age that they get into marriages that they openly or secretly regret. If after all your caution, you do get disappointment from an intimate relationship, learn from what happened and look forward to a better relationship in future.

As this is not a book about love and marriage, I will finish this chapter by stressing the main points, which is to have a focus, a clear destination, something that makes you want to get out of bed in the morning, something you feel passionate enough about to stay up late for, coffee or not. Your passion may be related to your strengths, your talents and your forte. You may think you already have all you want or be unintentionally enroute to that destination anyway, but it is worth taking some time to think about it and make it intentional, so that you can recognise when you get there. Happiness is not a destination, it is a choice. There is always room for improvement, so talking about issues helps you to reassess daily. Do not settle for an average life (whatever that is for you). You can have it all. Not by becoming too busy or ruthless, but by choosing your battles and taking one step at a time.

To the successful businessman who wants to have a better family life, to the happy family man who wants to start his own business, to the busy mother who wants more time to relax and enjoy her family, to the ambitious student who wants to get a distinction this year, to the unhappy lawyer thinking of a career change – **set your goal, have achievable targets and go for it!** You can start by reading something on the topic, using a diary effectively, cutting out irrelevant activities and unhelpful habits, or enrolling on a new course. If you really want to, you can do it. Reading this book is definitely a good start, but you have to be determined in yourself. Less talk, more thinking, more action.

Personal reflections and action plan

Chapter 2

One of the best ways for me to keep a check on myself and the things I do is to ask myself – "What is important today?"

What is important today may not have been important yesterday and may not be important next week, but thinking about what is important right now will help me to make a good decision about what to spend my time on. I organise fundraising events for a charity that helps young people in Africa. Some tasks are very time-specific. If I do not do them today, I will get a poorer or no result from doing it tomorrow. Although everyone likes the idea of 'not postponing till tomorrow what you can do today', I say, **"Do today what needs to be done today"**. If I can send those emails tomorrow and spend time with my daughter now, there is nothing wrong with leaving them till tomorrow if she needs me now. If I can postpone that meeting till tomorrow so I can apply for a government grant today, there is nothing wrong with that if applying tomorrow will be too late.

Time is limited so we have to choose wisely, because doing one thing might sometimes mean that another thing cannot get done today. If, for example, on a Friday afternoon, I have a lot of photocopying to do, but also have to make a few important official phone calls, it will be silly to choose to do the photocopying first, knowing that most offices close at 5pm and I can always do the photocopying later or get a secretary to do it. Some phone calls might not be urgent, but a phone call on Friday, in some situations, just might make the following week more productive than if you had left it till Monday morning. This sounds like common sense to most, but it is amazing how many times we get in a stressful mess because we did things in the wrong order and created avoidable problems. I know there are sometimes problems that arise despite being organised and sensible. These should be one-offs rather than the norm.

Some people get by with their poor decisions without creating any problems for themselves, but the sad thing is that they unknowingly miss out on opportunities due to poor time management. This is usually more obvious when it comes to deadlines. A man sees an email at the end of his lunch break advertising a job he thinks will be great for him. He marks it as 'unread' and decides he will apply later. He gets home at 6pm, has dinner and relaxation, then switches on the television. Three hours later, he is dozing off on the sofa and later drags himself to bed. He remembers the email during his coffee break at work the next day, sets a reminder to read it properly and apply that evening, then uses his lunch break to chat on the phone with a friend and gets home tired again at 6pm. He opens his email and gets distracted by a special offer email which led to him searching and booking unrelated flights for his next holiday. He is too tired to look at the job advert email again and keeps postponing it for another few days. By the time he finally reads the email properly, he finds he has now missed the application deadline and feels angry that he did not apply because it sounded like the perfect job for him. He will now never know what could have happened if he applied. He may have gotten a new and fantastic job, he may have only gotten to interview stage or he may have never received a reply – he will never know now.

Does this sound familiar? We tell ourselves, "Well, it was not meant to be", but is that really true? He had so many opportunities to act on the email if he really wanted to apply, but chose to do non-urgent tasks instead. No one was hurt by his decisions, but a series of episodes like this can seriously affect one's overall position and achievements in life. He could have woken up early one morning to complete the job application before work, knowing that he is normally tired after work. He could also have read the email properly at his lunchtime and made a plan of action once he knew what the deadline was. This kind of scenario happens every week with grant applications, job applications, discount offers, school applications, venue bookings etc. I personally feel that bad timing and lost opportunities can be avoided most times by forward planning and prioritization. I am not perfect at this, but I believe it is one of the ways I manage to get things done. I sometimes even have to do some things months in advance just because I have forecasted that I will not have time to do it when most people would be doing theirs. This just means that I may not seem to be relaxing as much when people would normally expect me to be, but I am happy and less stressed at busier periods.

The other thing to consider is – what will be important or what will have to be done *tomorrow*? How can I make my day easier tomorrow? This is a question I normally ask myself at the end of the day. As a mother, I honestly do not know how else to cope without this. It will be very difficult to get everyone out of the house in less than two hours on a weekday morning if I had not already done some of the preparation the night before. I am also grateful for a very helpful husband who understands how important this is and supports me. Getting ready for the next day includes simple things like getting clothes ready, thinking about meals for the day, what needs to go in our bags for what we are doing the next day and confirming appointments where necessary. The last thing you want is to wake up and realise that the feeding bottles have not been washed, there are not enough nappies for the day, the appointment letter I need cannot be found or there is not enough petrol in the car for where I need to be and I only have one hour to get ready because I took my time in bed not expecting to have these issues. Or worse still, getting a call from your child's school asking you to bring in something they really need because you forgot to put it in their bag during the morning rush, which just adds more pressure to your already cramped day!

I am not saying mistakes will not happen at times, but they are less likely to happen if we think about and plan even the smallest things in advance. Things sometimes do not go to plan and unexpected problems do arise, but at least it would not be as bad as if you had not made any preparation at all. Most problems depend on your perspective of them, and forward planning puts you in a better state of mind to deal with problems that arise. I find I am less able to deal with problems if I already feel unprepared and sloppy. There will be days when you are too tired to get things ready for the next day, but making a habit of preparing in advance, when possible, makes life easier and avoids unnecessary stress.

As an example, I once paid dearly for not properly reading our hotel reservation email in advance of a weekend away. We had a lovely day but had nowhere to sleep at night because we had missed the check-in time slot and had not even called the hotel in advance to let them know we might. We felt like the biblical Joseph and Mary that night with 'no room in the inn'. We had to sit in the car with a child, late at night, phoning different hotels to find a room for the night. It was a bank holiday weekend, and as you can imagine, most hotels were fully booked. I realised on that night how much our marriage had grown because we did not start fighting out of frustration as we would have done when we were younger. I am very impressed with my husband when I look back on that night because he dealt with the problem without blaming me or complaining. There could have possibly been another few hours or days of a 'post-fight atmosphere' in the family if we had argued, just because I did not prepare in advance (since I am normally the trip organiser in our family). Who know, maybe he was just too tired to argue at that time of the night! Eventually we found a nice hotel, more expensive than we would have normally gone for, but we were very grateful to have a room and not a stable! It was very annoying that we got charged for the room we did not stay in as well, but I accept responsibility for my mistake and have learnt from it.

Starting the day with an organised desk, clear plan and re-confirmed meetings can save a lot of time and energy. After a good day's work at the office, depending on what you do, it might be worth taking a few minutes to plan and prepare for the next day too. I remember doing this even as a junior doctor working on hospital wards. I believe this simple idea is sometimes the difference between good and average workers. Average is the one who always arrives two minutes late, rushing around, stressed and impatient, but gets the job done. They are always proud to say how many meals they missed, how many hours past closing time they stayed back to work and how many litres of coffee they had to drink to stay awake for that last meeting. Don't get me wrong, I sometimes have days like that, but those are not my best days.

If most of my days were like that, I would seriously reconsider my lifestyle. In fact, I think that people need to seriously reassess their working style and workload if they are *always* staying late to do what should be done within scheduled working hours.

I remember in my first year as a doctor, I found it very frustrating when I worked on wards where medical staff had made it the norm to leave late because they often stayed past closing time doing things that could have been done earlier in the day or handed over to the on-call doctor. It is not a secret that hospitals are commonly short-staffed, but staff need to be aware of their limitations for the sake of their health and wellbeing. Someone asked a doctor once if she was leaving early just because she finished at 5pm as expected! Should we really be expecting over-tired doctors to provide safe care? I know there were odd days when emergencies came up or when certain things would be better done by me (not the on-call doctor) after-hours for the sake of continuity, but apart from that, I think regular unscheduled overtime is not the mark of a good worker. I realised over the years that many regular over-timers somehow believed that staying late meant that they cared more. Some of them unfortunately had nothing much to go home to, and others just wanted to impress others with their apparent 'commitment' to the National Health Service. I would rather be a healthy, safe doctor who works efficiently and enjoys her job, to be honest.

I also found out that some workers stayed late because they spent more time socialising with colleagues at lunchtime or doing small tasks slowly because they accepted that staying late was normal. Most consultants agreed with me that regular overtime was not expected of junior doctors, but the reality was that unhealthy cultures had been created in some departments, so unfortunately leaving at 7pm was the norm for some. Working overtime was sometimes also due to poor prioritisation and inability to delegate or handover. I realised quickly as a doctor that there would always be more work to do, especially in a hospital, so I do my best for each day, handover or list jobs for myself for the next day, and go home to get some rest after my shift so that I did not get too stressed or unhappy with my job. While others had their coffee and wine to fall back on, I had to manage my time well to keep sane. Now that I manage a company too, I definitely still appreciate the worker that does a good job in the time paid for over the one who appears not be managing their time well.

Another question that is even more important than priorities for today and tomorrow is 'What is important for eternity?'. As human beings, we all have that need to live for something, to believe in something, to care about a cause. My friend, who is also a trustee of the charity I work for, is very passionate about orphans in Africa. Thankfully, she is also very good at fundraising so we have been able to help them through kind donations to the charity over the years. Even people who do not believe in God believe in something else, whether they recognise it or not. I think it is important to make a purposeful decision about what we believe in and what we are living for. Are we just like flowers, here today (beautiful and radiant), then gone tomorrow? Or is there a greater purpose for our existence? What is all this work and life about? In the end, does it really matter if you worked in a cafe, factory or bank? Does it matter if we have degrees, cars, houses, children or pets? **What would you do if no one was watching?** What are the friendships and relationships really about? Why are we such social beings with the need to love and be loved?

As intelligent people who like to plan our lives, careers, families and finances, I think it would be silly not to put some good thought into what the bigger picture really is. Like I said earlier, life is full of choices. Some things, such as our genotype and the circumstances we were born into, can be traced back to our parents, but most things are down to our own choices. They are usually 'modifiable' if we really want to change our lives. In medicine, we talk about non-modifiable and modifiable risk factors for disease. For example, gender and genetic predisposition to certain conditions are generally non-modifiable, but smoking status and obesity are risk factors for disease that we can try and change. Being aware of the non-modifiable factors can be seen as an advantage or disadvantage depending on the person. A man with a family history of diabetes can either try to live a healthy lifestyle to reduce his risk of developing it, or he may decide to take up unhealthy habits because he has concluded that he will get diabetes anyway! Some people hear the words "heaven and hell" and conclude that they might as well live carelessly because they are doomed for hell, while others hear that and take time to find out how they can get to spend eternity in heaven. There are also others who just bury their heads in the sand and refuse to make a firm decision about what they believe concerning life after death. **Sometimes refusing to make a decision is unfortunately equal to a negative choice.**

As you may have noticed, I like to be intentional in my life. Even when I do not understand politics and am not sure who to believe, I still pick up my pen, make a reasonable decision and vote. There is no neutral ground when it comes to the big questions of life. As a Christian, I believe that accepting Jesus (God's son) and living for Him guarantees me a place in heaven. Someone might read that and laugh, but I would rather live my life like there is a God and find out there isn't, than live my life like there isn't and find out there is. The big questions of faith and eternity are definitely worth making a serious decision about, so that the natural need to believe in something is met on purpose rather than just going wherever the wind blows and ending up in a mess one never imagined. I find that living with a purpose helps me to be more motivated and helps me through the challenges of life. My faith does not mean that everything will be easy, but it gives me the assurance that God has a bigger plan for my life which I aim to live out with His help. To be honest, without prayer and faith, I do not think that I would be where I am today. I have had difficult times that every drug put together would never have seen me through, but God has.

This is not a book about faith, but again I would summarise the main points by reminding you to evaluate what is truly important to you. What is important for today and tomorrow? What has to be done today and what can be done later? What can you do today to make tomorrow more productive? Are you missing opportunities due to procrastination and poor time management? You need to know what you aim to achieve in your 24 to 48 hours regularly, then it will make it easier to make decisions about how to spend your time. More importantly, the days and weeks run into years, which make up our lifetime. What is your overall purpose in life? What will truly be important in eternity? Do you need to explore this further and give it more thought? What will still matter after we all die? What guides your secret thoughts and actions?

I love helping young people mainly because they will most likely be here after we are gone, and inspiring them to achieve great things with their lives is worth more than any money you could give them. It is exciting to see people live up to their full potential and achieve their dreams, without being held back by challenges and ignorance. What are your core values?

What do you get really excited about? Do your friends and inner circles know and reflect that? Energy and time can be wasted through lack of direction. The way people spend their time and money is the greatest reflection of their values and priorities. If someone says that they really value family, for example, but there is no sign of that when you watch them, they are just deceiving themselves. We need to be intentional about our choices, values and beliefs, with a view of eternity, so that after all is said and done, there will be no regrets at the end of our lives.

Personal reflections and action plan

Chapter 3

Everyone wants to be successful, but what does that really mean? Is it the wealthy man in London who has everything at his fingertips and several fat bank accounts? Is it the famous singer who cannot go anywhere without being recognised? Is it the posh woman who has three well-behaved children in private school, a rich loving husband and two dogs? Is it the nice young man who has a stunning girlfriend that would do anything for him? Is it the professional runner who has a healthy lifestyle and several gold medals? Is it the beautiful girl who won a beauty contest, swimming competition and national physics quiz competition in the same month? Is it the young woman who has already travelled to thirty countries and worked in ten orphanages at only twenty-five? Is it the businessman who doubles his profits every month and opens a new branch of his store every year? Is it the employee who has worked in the same company for the past thirty years and is now a director? Is it the man who helps everyone, has no points on his driver's license and gives half his income to charity? Or is it the old man who discovered the cure for a deadly disease and saved millions of lives as a missionary?

Success in life is an interesting concept. It is defined differently by everyone depending on what they want out of life. Having your own clear definition for success is important. This removes the need to compare yourself to others. For example, if I feel that having a job with a six figure salary defines success for me, I will not be bothered by the runner who ran five miles in five minutes! If I feel success is having two happy children and a handsome husband, I would not be bothered by the surgeon who does seven kidney transplants a week. If success means having a small house, no boss and running my own business – no matter how small, then an offer of a job in Washington with fantastic benefits would not move me. In fact, defining success for yourself helps you to find role models and learn from them, so that instead of feeling jealous of the man who has the great career you fancy, you can read his biography or talk to him for some advice. There is enough room in the world for everyone to be successful and happy, because we all have different personalities and desires.

It is sad that some people do not have a clear concept of what success is for them, so they cannot be proud of their own achievements. They look around criticizing other people's lives and are unable to commend people's good work because they are constantly comparing themselves to others. They are sometimes jealous and negative, even when they should be humbling themselves to learn more and get advice from others. People who have no success stories of their own might look at others who are successful in certain areas and belittle their efforts with silly remarks. When they see something they would like to achieve, they find excuses for not doing it, and even find fault with the lifestyles of those that have achieved it. When they eventually stumble on success, they are unable to own, appreciate and celebrate it, because they have said horrible things about similar success in other people's lives.

A typical example would be a struggling hairdresser who makes jokes about a cleaner, belittling the effort she puts into her work, saying that anyone could do it. The same hairdresser then sees a journalist and criticizes her for being a 'career woman', assuming she has no time for family and calls her "stuck up". When the same hairdresser meets a very successful hairdresser, she chooses to focus on her idea that the hairdresser is 'too posh' and misses the opportunity to get helpful tips to help her become more successful in that area too. **It takes an intelligent person to recognise the wisdom they need in someone else and ask for it.** With the right attitude, the hairdresser in this example could probably learn more about attention to detail from the cleaner, time management from the journalist and networking from the successful hairdresser.

We need to realise that although the world seems to be in competition, the happiest people do not compare themselves to others. We all have different paths and different stories. **If I must compare myself to someone, let it be me.** I should strive to be a better person than I was yesterday. Understand that other people's success will not prevent you from achieving yours. Even if they are in the same profession, job or class, I believe there is enough room for everyone to be successful if we are true to ourselves, because success means different things to different people, and life is made up of ups and downs for everyone. I remember my father used to encourage me to aim to improve my final total marks at school every term, even when I was already the best in the class. That really helped me to understand the importance of improving myself no matter what others were doing.

The child who struggles with Mathematics and gets a 'B' should be able to celebrate that success as much as a child who got an 'A'. A student who got another distinction (with a total score that is less than what he had last year) may not be pleased with that, while a student who aimed for and got a C could be over the moon at his success. If both students compare themselves to each other, the student with the A might deny himself greater success by feeling that he is better than the C student and need not do more, while the C student might be unable to celebrate his achievement because he feels he needs to get an A. If the C student keeps on improving, as he should, he too will get an A someday, but if the A student becomes comfortable where he is, he might just end up with a B soon.

In essence, we all have different capabilities and different challenges which affect our outcomes in life. An immigrant who works hard to get to the highest social class in society has overcome much more challenges and shown more tenacity than the man who was born into a rich home and remains at the same level in which the immigrant has now found himself. If the immigrant understands that he is not in competition with anyone but himself, he will keep moving up till he reaches his highest potential with the resources available to him. The other man will be foolish to compare himself to this immigrant because they obviously have not had the same journey and probably have differing goals in life. He may choose to commend the immigrant for making headway in life despite his challenges, or he may choose to call the immigrant a greedy workaholic. On one hand, he could have learnt a few things from the hardworking immigrant, but has lost the opportunity because of his bad attitude. On the other hand, he may be truly content with his life and actually feel that working for more would be greed, but he should still be able to commend the hardworking man without feeling the need to criticize his achievements. This is not to say that people who appear to be rich do not have challenges. The point is that people should run their own race to achieve their own definition of success, without feeling belittled by or they themselves belittling others.

If we know what we want out of life, we are more able to celebrate our achievements and be happy for others too. When I was younger, many girls dreamt about marrying a rich man so they would not have to lift a finger to work. As much as I also enjoy that fantasy, I know for sure that I enjoy working and would be very unhappy if I was not allowed to. This means that I can be happy for a friend who actually prefers not to work, without feeling the need to compare her life to mine or belittle her life as a housewife. If she is truly happy with her life, she will be able to celebrate my successes with me too without feeling the need to make me feel guilty about working outside my home. Most negative talk arises when people are not happy with their own lives, refuse to do something about it, but try to make others feel bad so they can feel better. I think part of living a happy life is to recognise those issues early on and remove yourself from jealous, controlling, stagnant and negative people. Wisdom is needed here to discern whether the words we did not want to hear were said to help, control or damage us. People that make one feel inadequate and unworthy of happiness should not be seen often because they soon drain the energy out of you, but **if there is a correction to be received in their nasty words, do not miss it because of the packaging**. It is important to surround ourselves with people who can inspire, encourage and understand us, so that we are not expending energy trying to prove how good or likeable we are.

Obviously, there will be situations where it is difficult to avoid such people. For example – a colleague at work who gossips and criticises others all the time, a spouse who was brought up that way, or a parent who is lonely and frustrated. It can be difficult to get out of seeing or hearing such a person often if you have strong ties. I deal with such issues by speaking out more so that my positive talk will overcome the negative. It is sometimes easier to stay quiet and passively agree when around negative people, but their words are like rocks that pile up in your mind, leaving you feeling heavy and uneasy, especially if you are not a negative and critical person yourself. It may be hard to get a word in with some people, but it is worth making the effort to say your mind, so that you **become the influencer rather than the receiver. Direct the conversations where you want them to go.** Steer away from topics that usually 'get them going' in a bad way and focus on positive, happy topics. Soon, you will see that they either cut down their negative talk generally or just to you. They may also just find someone else to pour it on. Hopefully, your positive actions, which speak louder than words, will inspire them to re-evaluate their lifestyle and change. Those that refuse to change will somehow fit into a redefined relationship with you if the connection is valuable to them too.

Even when two people are both striving for the same goals (as most friends and colleagues would be), it is possible to be happy for each other and avoid comparing ourselves to one another. For example, if a friend and I both run businesses and feel that more customers is a measure of success for us both, we can share ideas and try to succeed together. After all, for most businesses, there will be enough customers out there for more than one company. If business people realise that customers have minds of their own to be able to choose where to go, we will accept that there will be good and bad days for every business, so overall, it is possible for us all to succeed. **Good success does not require any sabotage.**

Once you have decided what success means for you – work towards it. It does not just happen! Unless, of course, you do not wish to do better than you are doing right now. A musical band that wants worldwide success cannot just sit at home and expect it to happen. They need to work on their music, image and publicity, among other things. As resources are limited, they will need to be organised and consider how much time, money and effort to invest in all areas that need to be improved to achieve this aim. If they get national fame and are still serious about their initial definition of success, they will keep working hard to become internationally known. They should be able to pause and celebrate the little successes on the way to their big dream, but must keep their eyes on the goal if they are to achieve it. This is not to say that they cannot change their minds when the reality of fame at a national level sets in and probably feels too much. People sometimes wish for things without knowing what it truly involves, which is why it is important to find out what it really involves before we invest too much and realise we never wanted it. I have heard of doctors that spend years training in specialties that they feel are impressive, only to drop out and start afresh in a 'less glamorous' specialty when they realise they cannot keep up the act. Hopefully, they learn from the experience and do not become bitter professionals. I find it inspiring to hear of celebrities that started building on their talent from a young age. Whether it was their dream or a parent's, someone worked hard to achieve it. Some people dream of fast money and quick fame, but you will notice that those that do not work for what they have are usually not able to keep it. This is why it is very easy for a lottery millionaire to go back into debt due to poor management of their finances. **The struggles and even failures on the road to success make us more equipped to handle the success when we have it.**

What can make a man leave home at 5am and go to bed at 12am for little obvious reward? The biggest motivation for people is their vision. If he believes that doing this now will get him the job, status, fame, satisfaction or life he always dreamed of, he will do it. A man with no vision will never understand why someone would work that hard for anything. When you imagine yourself twenty years from now, where do you see yourself? What are you doing now to make it happen? What can you do now to make it happen? What are you doing now to make it less likely to happen? Some people choose the path of least resistance, expect little out of life and hope to just get by. You get what you expect. The sad reality is that if you are not moving forward, you are definitely moving backward.

There is no standing still in life. A primary school child can one day be the boss of her teacher if the teacher does not keep improving herself. Yes, experience cannot be bought, but wisdom is so much more than age. If the teacher is genuinely happy with her life and really does not desire more than that, then she will be happy and proud of her pupil who one day becomes head teacher. If she stays the same over the years due to laziness and lack of vision, she will either resign due to pride or become a difficult member of staff to deal with when her pupil becomes her boss. Like I say to my young listeners when giving inspirational talks in schools, "If you become a doorman, just make sure you are the best doorman there is, and that it was intentional and not because you could not be bothered to study and improve yourself."

What makes a well-paid dentist buy a cheap second-hand car and live in a small flat when he can afford more? Vision! If he feels that he would rather sacrifice his comfort for now in order to invest in a business, support a charity, send his children to better schools or save for a mansion, he will do this without complaining. His vision will keep him comforted when he meets friends with expensive cars and houses, which they probably pay for by instalment, just to keep up with the Jones'. Again, having your own definition of success helps you to be happy for others while being content with your own life.

His friends might actually already be living the life of their dreams within their means, but this dentist might be looking forward to his celebration of success in future when his son graduates from the best school, or when his business employs more people than the National Health Service or when he sees a whole city changed through the work of his charity or when he has finished building that amazing mortgage-free mansion he always wanted. The only mistake here would be to wait till then to be happy. Happiness is a choice we must go for everyday. No one can guarantee tomorrow, so **we should try to enjoy the journey as much as the destination.**

I remember thinking how much happier I would feel when I got pregnant, then how happy I would be when I have the baby, then how happy I would be when she is walking, then how happy I would be when she can do more things for herself! We all like to have something to look forward to but we have to remind ourselves that **life is happening now and we must enjoy the moments.** I am glad I learnt this while I still have my children at home. They soon grow up and leave the nest. I really enjoyed the first few weeks after the birth of my first child. It was a very special time for my family, which made our marriage stronger. Despite the night feeds, tears (both mine and baby's!) and steep learning curve, we were able to share many special moments that cannot be put into words. I especially remember taking my time to wash the baby, sing to her and talk to her in the mornings after my husband left for work. We would then do her feeds, go for walks and do nappy changes throughout the day, which surprisingly made the hours pass quickly. I would usually make sure the baby and house were clean in time for my husband's return so that we could enjoy the evening together. As a woman who likes to have a plan, I was very happy that our baby got into a good feeding and sleep routine from her early days so we could still enjoy our evenings as a couple. Even with a healthy child – thank God – I still had to take time to study my baby and know how best to care for her. She was not my patient, not my niece and not my friend's baby. She is *my daughter*. I knew it was my special role as her mother to understand and care for her, but I am so glad she has a very good father to help too!

Even with a thing like having a baby, I had a vision of what kind of family life I wanted, and found out what we needed to do to achieve it. This is obviously a work in progress. **Sometimes, a vision needs to be shared so that others can help to achieve it.** No man is an island, and it is good to be able to give and receive help. You can get drained if you are always giving, but you can become a burden if you are always receiving. Everyone has something to give. Even the helpless one-day-old baby was able to give me rest when she had a good sleep! On the other hand, there will be some that take from you in the pretence of giving. Those are the ones to be aware of, so that we can manage our time and emotional resources wisely. There is nothing wrong with 'giving' in such circumstances, but the danger is that your time is not recognised as a gift so you get stressed wondering why you are so tired. There were times as a new mother that I had to ask friends to visit at another more convenient time, because their visit (gift) could become stressful if I was not mentally prepared for it. As much as I loved people coming to spend time with me and the baby in the first few days, I was very aware of the fact that parenting was all new to us and we would need some space to get our heads around caring for a new baby. Thankfully, we had sensible friends, who always checked before popping in, and close friends that knew when to just drop a gift, check on us quickly and leave. Even during maternity leave, I had a diary to plan my days so that I could spread out the visits, activities and alone times, so I was never overwhelmed or lonely. I learnt so much about myself in this period and even applied some managerial skills to my home life to be able to continue to keep things calm and happy, which is my vision for my home.

People who have a clear vision are not worried about people-pleasing or what 'people' will say. They are able to respectfully say 'yes' or 'no', as required, without letting others control or manipulate them. It is important to always remember that **we are not responsible for other people's happiness.** You could bend over backwards a million times to please, but people will still find something to criticise you for, if they want to. People that like you will not need convincing to do so, people that don't will always find a reason not to. Loving someone does not necessarily mean liking them. Some people just love to have something to complain about. This is sometimes due to idleness, inferiority complex, loneliness, worthlessness, their need for control or lack of autonomy. We cannot feel responsible for or try to make up for the way others choose to live their lives – it is their choice. If you are usually helpful and kind, sensible people will not take offence when you are unable to oblige them, because you have other priorities at the time.

Having a clear vision and definition of success saves you time, money and energy; because you will not waste time stressing over issues and drama that does not help your vision. Surrounding yourself with the right people can make even the toughest challenges easier to conquer. The tricky thing is choosing who the right people are for each season of life and finding ways to politely reduce your contact with people who are not right for your progress.

Personal reflections and action plan

Chapter 4

It is interesting how people seem to fall in one of two camps: the dependent and the independent, as I call them. The first group of people – the dependents – feel that everyone owes them something and they should be cared for. They express this in a wide spectrum of attitudes and behaviour. Some adults have this attitude towards their parents, siblings or friends, while others have this childish attitude towards their employers, landlords or even the government. They want people to always do things for them and they feel helpless without other people sorting out their problems.

Most people know someone like this. It could be the grown man who won't find a job and leave his mother's house, or the grown woman who feels that she has more right to her brother's wealth than his wife and children, or the friend who is always asking for favours and never seems to be able to get on their own two feet to build an admirable life of their own. Some people may not be so obvious in their 'dependence mentality', but their attitudes show that this is the mentality they have. They feel that getting help from friends and family is their right, and often get offended when people are not able to offer it. They are very ungrateful when help or gifts do not meet their expectations, and they find it difficult to put themselves in someone else's shoes, because they are too busy thinking about their own needs. They feel that other people's lives are better than theirs, despite the fact that they are unwilling to work harder or endure little hardships to get what they want. People like this only hear what they want to hear and cannot be reasoned with when they want something, because they cannot see beyond their own desires.

Another type of dependence mentality is towards 'outsiders'. Sometimes, people form alliances in this. They complain about the 'outsider' for years without making any progress in their own lives because of such a negative mentality. We have all had or contributed to conversations like this at one point or another in our lives. The dependent mentality here is usually towards a superior of some sort. Superiority could be real or perceived, but people with this mentality generally have a negative view of the superior/outsider because they feel they are not getting what they deserve from them. This could be a tenant who always complains about his/her landlord, always asking for more from them, while making little or no effort to take good care of the property he/she lives in. I believe strongly that people reap what they sow. If you do not look after someone else's property, how can you hope to own yours one day? Even if you eventually do, you will most probably not be able to care for it well, or you might end up with wicked tenants too!

Some have a dependent mentality towards their employers. They are never satisfied with any effort made for them. They complain about the wages, the benefits, the office space, the holidays, the policies, the workload, the hours, the location, the processes and even the job itself. The way some people talk, it is hard to understand why they still work there! They want the boss to grant their every request, give them more this and more that, without stopping to consider how their requests or attitudes may be affecting the business. People with this mentality never really care about the progress of the company or the stress they themselves may be causing the management. They find it hard to see things from a different perspective because they have unfounded grudges against all 'fat cats', including the one that employs them! Some are so neck deep in this 'dependent' mentality that they constantly wish their employers bad, without realising that the downfall of their employer or boss could have a negative impact on them too! They want more money, more benefits, more paid holiday, but are not willing to give more to the company in any way. The 'dependent' employees are usually the ones with the highest number of work absences, and they need the most motivation and input from management to do the jobs they are being paid for. Other employees that work hard and get promotions soon become disliked along with the employer, because 'Ms Dependent' just hates anyone in authority, especially if they do not approve the inconsiderate leave and pay rise she requested.

The biggest 'outsider' that people can have a dependent mentality towards is the government. People can have hours of conversation on what the government could be doing better. We criticise national and local government leaders with such passion sometimes that I wonder why we do not run for the leadership posts ourselves since we know so much better! People want less tax and more benefits, less regulations and more protection. We want laws that make life so easy for us personally, without thinking of how it will affect another group in the same country. We conveniently forget too that government money spent on one thing means less money for another. In some countries, the dependent mentality leads some people into high levels of corruption, where they take advantage of the respectable posts they have to use government resources for personal gain without thought for how this affects the society in general. People find it easy to blame the government when they do not have a job, blame the government when their business fails, and blame the government even when their own children fail or become wayward! Where is the sense of personal responsibility in that? Is the government really responsible for the fact that you only applied for only one percent of the jobs you could have applied for before giving up? Is the government really responsible for the fact that you did not perform good market research before starting your business? Is the government really responsible for the fact that you send your children to school and never make time to check on their progress? It is easy to forget that the government provides funding for schools, business grants, student loans and childcare vouchers when complaining, forgetting also that there are similar people abroad who do not even have these social benefits. No government is without its flaws, but there cannot be progress if all we do is complain. As the famous saying goes, "Ask not what your country can do for you, but what you can do for your country".

There is nothing wrong in expecting things from people, especially where they have clear responsibility for that. It is not unreasonable for a citizen to expect good governance, a child to expect provision from parents, an employee to expect fair treatment from their employer or friends to expect support from each other. The bad 'dependent' mentality, in my opinion, is where people only want to take, take and take but not to give. Everyone has something to give; the question is whether they are willing.

There is another type of personality I describe as the 'independents'. They are usually strong characters who feel that they do not need anyone. Sometimes, if you look closely enough, they are actually weak people pretending to be strong. They push people away with their words and/or actions, believing that success is only good when achieved alone. They are difficult to work with in a team because they either want to do it all alone, or show no interest in the task if it is not going their way. They find it hard to ask for help or receive gifts. They do not expect good from anyone and feel the need to repay every favour. You give them a gift and they bring out their wallet to pay you for it, you give them a lift and they want to pay for the petrol, you take them out for a meal and they want to split the bill, you help them mow their lawn and they want to come over and do yours next week! It is good to be aware of and grateful for favours, but I think it is sad when people cannot accept a real gift with a simple "Thank you" and move on. Sometimes it is because people were brought up to never take something for nothing, and sometimes bad life experiences have made them to believe that nothing good is truly free. The 'dependents' can learn something from this group because the 'dependents' seem to expect everything to be free and sometimes even forget to pay for things or return things that were 'borrowed'! In the same way, the 'independents' need to learn to accept help because "no man is an island".

Even though it seems that many people fall into the 'dependent' or 'independent' group, I think that the best way to be is 'interdependent', as psychologists describe it. It is good to know when you need help and how to ask for it. It is also good to know how to see things from other people's perspective, to be understanding when they cannot help you and offer them your help when you can. Offering help is sometimes as simple as being considerate with your boss, being flexible for your employer, volunteering your services to help the society and government, using your skills/profession to help society, sorting out a small issue in your rented house before it becomes a big problem for your landlord, getting a job and supporting or relieving your elderly parents financially, offering to help siblings with childcare etc. without waiting to be asked, just being a faithful friend to your sibling or even visiting that friend who is always the one driving to yours.

Life is much less stressful when people have an attitude of service instead of pride. Pride is what makes one to expect everyone else to do things for them, while they have no space in their thoughts for the needs of others. Pride is also what makes someone feel that he/she can do everything and does not need anyone's help. As I said before, we can *have* it all, but we cannot *do* it all. Even the most successful people (however you define success) constantly need to delegate or accept favours from others. At a time when I was very busy with different aspects of my life and foresaw that I would end up struggling or falling behind on my commitments, I prayed for a helper for my charity work. I think that year was probably the best year we had as a charity up to that time because of the wonderful help I got from a friend. Involving others brings in different skills and perspectives to make projects grow and flourish. Every small business owner will also know the value of interdependence, because most people have to start with the support of friends and family. On one hand, a business owner who gives so much without receiving will end up stressed or bankrupt. On the other hand, a business owner who uses people for his own gain, without giving back will end up alone and miserable.

I think the best example of interdependence for me is in marriage. It is really funny to hear married women singing 'independent woman' songs. First of all, you and your spouse depend on each other at least for emotional support and physical satisfaction; otherwise, it is hardly a marriage. You may have all the money in the world and never need to discuss purchases with your spouse, but the reality is that the outcome of any financial decision you make will affect you both, as long as you are married, so it is wise to work together in that area too. Interdependence is not about having an intimate marriage-like relationship with everyone around you, but it is the understanding that **you are part of a big engine, which works better because you are in it, but is also there to serve you.**

We will have different levels of relationship with different people. If we take time to understand people and how to interact with them as individuals, we are more likely to have a more peaceful life. Understanding people will help you to know what you can expect of whom, who you can trust with what and where to draw the lines. When we delegate or ask for help, we need to be able to trust people to do a good job; otherwise we might as well do it ourselves! This trust only comes from knowing people and that happens when we invest the time and the mental effort to understand them. It will be stupid to trust a toddler to do my taxes. At the same time, it will be just as stupid to spend time figuring out how to do my accounts if I have an accountant working as a receptionist in my company. Interdependence works better when we are willing to share our skills and experiences for the good of each other.

I have learnt in life that there are people who think it is smart to hide their resources while using yours as well. Somehow they think they can get ahead in life by taking from others and adding to theirs, without sharing. For me, they fall into the 'dependent' group and I try to give them only as much of my time and energy as I can spare. Realising that I am giving 100% in a partnership, while someone else is being secretive and parasitic by giving me only 10% of themselves (pretending to be the one in need) does not particularly motivate me to put them in the top of my priority list of people to visit on a weekend!

Interacting with people who are not as 'privileged' as you helps you to be more grounded and grateful for what you have. This does not mean looking down on them to make yourself feel better, but being a true friend to help them however you can. Help does not always have to be financial. Time, connections and information can be more valuable than cash hand-outs, sometimes. I have found over the years that they too would have also helped you through that friendship in priceless ways.

I can never put into words the joy I get from helping young people through my charity work and the satisfaction I get from helping someone who is ill, as a healthcare professional. Some of the greatest lessons I have learnt in life have been from the most unexpected places. I have also learnt that having good intentions does not mean that you will not get hurt. In fact, it makes the offence more hurtful when you were only there to be helpful or to offer friendship. This is all part of understanding people and what you can trust them with. Some people can be trusted with trivial information or jobs, while others, who always understand, defend and support you, can be trusted with the most sensitive information and tasks. It is only experience from a relationship with them that differentiates the two groups. You will be hurt when you trust someone that did not deserve to be trusted, but there should always be room for forgiveness when you feel it was a mistake and not a reflection of their true character. If you are convinced that this is really a revelation of their true character, it is best to forgive and move on from that level of closeness with them to avoid more devastating betrayals.

In all our self-preservation, we must make sure we are not punishing others for the mistakes of people in our past. Life becomes very difficult when we try to judge people based on the actions of others. A woman who is harsh with her husband, because she feels her kind mother was treated badly in her own marriage, is never going to have a happy marriage.

A girl who refuses to trust any man, because her ex-boyfriend cheated on her, is only giving her ex-boyfriend more power to hurt her by stopping her from enjoying a good relationship. A man who keeps his father-in-law at arm's length, because of the stories he heard about controlling fathers-in-law, is only depriving himself of a potentially good relationship, based on assumptions. A business-owner who refuses to hire black people, because he had a bad experience with an African in the past, is missing out on great staff due to his prejudice. Some people are better kept at arm's length, but that should not apply to 'all others like them'. We cannot let one person's bad character change our good personality. Interdependence means we are constantly involved with others, so we need to try and keep all our relationships as stress-free and cordial as possible. Even the worst person to you today can be of help some day.

I find that when I make the effort to talk to people and get to know them, I learn something new. The problem is usually that I did not get to know them in the first place because we seemed to have very different interests and personalities. Talking to them helps to broaden my knowledge and makes me more likely to be that admirable lady that 'has a solution or knows someone for every problem' when I am older. I'm sure we all like to know people like that – people that seem to know something about everything or at least have the number of someone who will be able to solve any problem you discuss with them. I must admit that speaking to people who have completely different interests and lifestyles sometimes makes me feel stupid, but I do not mind looking stupid to gain more knowledge in my quest for interdependence and a well-rounded life.

Talking to certain people and watching the way they choose to live their lives can be frustrating and annoying though. Yes, I do get irritated by certain things, especially when I feel that people should know better. As I grow older, I find that it is best to keep my opinion to myself with these kinds of people, unless it is asked for. It is more important to maintain a peaceful relationship, so that they are able to ask for my opinion when they want it and I am able to receive help from them, through a good relationship, if I need it. A lot of people who have lifestyles I do not agree with probably know everything I was about to tell them anyway, but they still choose to live their lives in a way that seems careless or dangerous to me. The best way to produce a positive change is by being a good example with a non-judgemental attitude.

As an 'interdependent' woman, I am aware of the risk of possibly being influenced by my frequent exposure to people with lifestyle choices I do not believe are right, so I try to keep contact to a minimum so that I am not too irritated or influenced negatively. **You save yourself a lot of stress when you stop trying to change people, accept them for who they are and wisely manage your own emotions regarding them.**

Sometimes with proper reflection, you may find that they were right anyway, and you were only irritated because you did not really understand a better way of doing things at the time. No one is beyond learning. If we keep our minds open to learning and change, we will always end up better than we started. We cannot control people's words and actions, but we can certainly control our reactions to them. We can also control how much of it we take. I will not sit and listen to someone insult me daily, just because I am able to control myself from punching them. As a grown woman, I will take myself out of the situation in order to keep my peace and sanity. Surely, prolonged periods of internal conflict, trying to resist the urge to give someone a piece of my mind, cannot be good for my stress levels!

Finally, for this chapter, I would like to say something about being generous with encouragement and compliments. It is no good thinking how wonderful someone is, without telling them. Remember that we all need each other. Be grateful for all you get and give no place to pride. Be clear about who you are, what you will or will not do, so that people around you know what they can expect. If people know that you are a person of integrity, who gives and accepts help, has their priorities in order, expects the best of others but makes allowances for their shortcomings, is able to forgive and move on, is able to face issues and give a clear opinion when asked, does not try to control and change others, and is not afraid to learn and change for the better, you will have less things to worry about, because the 'dependents' will know that you cannot be manipulated, and the 'independents' will respect you.

Personal reflections and action plan

Chapter 5

One of the most important questions we need to be able to answer in life is "Who am I?". Just take a minute to answer that in less than ten words.

Who are you? How do you define yourself and how do you want others to define you? What is the most important part of your identity? For example, are you a married lawyer or a lawyer who is married? Are you an Irish doctor or a doctor who is Irish? Are you a working parent or a parent who works? I realise that life is not that clear-cut and people are not so easily defined. The woman in front of you could be a mother, sister, daughter, friend, fiancée, employee, volunteer, buddhist, designer, role model and sponsor. That man in your office could be a director, father, son, brother, pianist, engineer, singer, husband, friend, pastor and student. With so many facets to our lives, it is hard to define yourself in less than ten words, while giving enough weight to the most important aspects of your life. Basically, you can define yourself however you wish, or even choose not to define yourself in words. You can define yourself differently in different scenarios or choose to stick to one definition wherever you are asked. The most important thing is to know for yourself who you are and be true to that.

It is only when you know your worth that you are able to value yourself and **expect respect** from others. It breaks my heart to see people that get into a poverty mind-set and slave mentality due to their own beliefs. They believe that they have no control over their circumstances and begin to act accordingly. They let people talk to them rudely, never stand up for their rights and always expect the worst. I believe that we need to value ourselves and define what is okay by us for us. Even a child born last year exhibits a strong will and can let you know what he/she wants or does not want. Whether it is a sensible choice or not, is another matter! It seems that somewhere along the line, life beats that self-worth out of some of us and we begin to feel that we must 'go with the flow' and accept whatever is thrown our way. This starts to happen slowly when we easily accept defeat instead of trying again (and again, and again) to achieve success. 'Growing up' sometimes sadly also involves giving up on our dreams for a more 'realistic' view of life, based on other people's expectations and experiences, forgetting that we are all different.

I remember sometimes feeling different in saying that I wanted to become a doctor when there were no medical doctors in my family. Thankfully, my parents supported me with that vision. All the encouragement I got as a child helped me to see beyond the challenges, and has also taught me the importance of saying positive things to young people, because not everyone is privileged to have a supportive family. As a teenager or adult, you can choose to focus on the negative words spoken in your past or decide to fill your mind with new and positive words that will encourage you for the future. There are several motivational talks and books out there for anyone who needs to start afresh in their thinking. Reading this book is a good start, but unfortunately, renewing your mind is not a quick job. You need to hear something over and over again until you believe it, so that your new positive thoughts begin to show in your words and actions. Most people say that 'seeing is believing', but in my experience, you sometimes need to believe even before you can see. Most successful people today did not start believing in their achievements (e.g. company, project, career, family, product etc.) after it materialised. They put in the work because they believed in it and that is why we all see it today.

If you consider your life to be a project, what would you call it? What is it worth and what investments do you need to make? People spend years preparing and training to become professionals, how much more effort should we put into our personal lives, happiness and future? If you define yourself using your past experiences, you leave no room for growth and development. It is just like a child defining herself as a helpless baby just because she once was! It would also sound crazy if she described herself as a powerful woman just because she hopes to achieve that one day. In my perspective, a good definition of oneself should include their roots, present journey and future destination. That would obviously be difficult to put into a sentence, and does not need to be. What matters more is the realisation of who you are, your self-worth and expectations from life.

There is a big difference between knowing your worth and being an arrogant person. For example, an arrogant person will talk down at people, but a person who values him/herself will not be spoken to in that manner and will not speak condescendingly to others either. You can only love others as much as you love yourself. Someone who thinks it is okay to talk to people in such a way must somehow believe that someone 'superior' to him/her is allowed to speak to them in that manner too. There are classic examples of this in some hierarchical jobs or institutions, where people feel that it is part of the journey to the top to be treated worse than an animal. While it may be difficult to take a stand in some situations, I believe there is always one way or another to make it known that you value yourself and are not there to be abused. Sometimes, it is in the way that you comport yourself, your polite but firm responses, use of initiative and your actions. There will be times when intentional discussions must be had or even formal complaints will have to be made, without fear. There are other times when you need to decide on purpose to overlook certain unacceptable behaviours for a greater purpose. If, for example, you choose to tolerate an arrogant boss's behaviour in order to gain a qualification you need for the next step in your career, do not go around complaining to everyone else about it and getting yourself into a slavery mindset. Remember that it was your choice to stay there and go for that job/qualification. You could have chosen to leave or to speak to him directly about it, but accepting such behaviour is a choice, so **stop moaning and focus on the prize.**

It is very sad when people take on the helpless role, accepting no responsibility or control for their lives, and always waiting for someone else to save them. Most people are blessed to not really be in a helpless situation, it is just that they refuse to see the choices they have and take responsibility for the path they have chosen. If people take some time to think of those children who really have no choice or control over what happens to them, or the people in real, unavoidable problems and persecution, they would stop moaning so much about their own lives. How can a man with two hands, two feet, a functioning brain and whatever job/income, complain more than someone who lives in an unstable economy with disability, absolute poverty and no security? The man with a job can choose to find another job, start his own business, retrain in another profession or live on less money if he truly felt that sad about his life and job! Why is there too much talk and no action? I think it is because people do not value their life and time as much as they should. If we all realise that our days become our years and life, then we would be quick to change what saddens us in the best way we can, rather than complaining without any improvement.

Changing your circumstances may not always be possible, but you can always change your attitude. For example, an overweight woman can choose to love her size twenty clothes, or decide to eat less and exercise more to see the weight loss she desires. There is no point in complaining all the time about being big, getting depressed about it, lying to your doctor about your snacking habits, eating the same food portions as thin people and expecting the weight to drop magically. I remember how hard it was to get back into exercise after having my baby, but I did it because I really wanted to. I remember motivating myself to go to the gym by preparing educational talks, movies or music I could listen to while on the treadmill. I am also fortunate to have a husband who enjoyed bonding with the baby while I was out. I might have had to pay for a babysitter otherwise. The important thing is to decide how important exercise is to you, and make it happen.

Good health is not just about looking well, but also feeling good mentally and spiritually. For me, the order of importance is spiritual and mental, then physical. The order may be different for you but they are all important because spiritual and mental illness can manifest as physical illness, which we all dread. Like most people, I could definitely do more for my physical health. My usual joke is about how unfit I am, but I think that defining myself and what gives me happiness, helps me to balance my time out so that I am reasonably happy with all aspects of my life. This means that I may be average in some areas, but I am happy in all.

I learnt from a work colleague how she makes physical exercise a part of her family's routine so that the children grow up to see exercise as something to enjoy and not something to dread. That really motivated me to review our family time and how best to include physical activities that will improve us all in this area. Eating, talking, laughing and learning together is good and comes naturally to us, but I feel that coming out of our comfort zone to exercise and get fit together will be good for us. We decided to start slow by going for walks or dance together, which I believe can lead to other fun activities as the children grow older. It is not always easy to build new habits, but perseverance and commitment makes it possible. This is why it is important to surround oneself with positive and forward-thinking people. Go where you are appreciated and not tolerated. This does not mean creating a false, perfect image of yourself where you cannot be free to make mistakes and learn. We all enjoy praise and encouragement, but we must not love flattery to the detriment of our need for correction from time to time. Good friends/family are those that can sensitively point out areas that need improvement without making you feel less loved or valued. Knowing yourself will then help you to digest any criticism without getting offended, make any adjustments that need to be made and move on from it a better person.

As my husband likes to say, "Life is not that difficult". We are all here to help each other, but how can others help you if you do not know what help you require? Take time to study yourself. What makes you happy, what makes you stressed, what makes you sad, what makes you angry, what makes you efficient, what makes you slow? Armed with such knowledge, you can quickly read situations to know how best to react. Knowing myself has helped me many times to manage my emotions in situations where I can see that there is a factor which I already know is likely to make me feel stressed or angry. Sometimes it is not possible to remove stressful or annoying factors, but the awareness of them helps us to manage situations more maturely with better outcomes. Knowledge of myself has also helped me to predict potentially stressful circumstances and avoid them by doing things differently. It is funny how we take time to study spouses, colleagues and friends to get the best out of those relationships, but hardly put thought into discovering our own selves. We are sometimes surprised when people tell us things about ourselves, and can be even more surprised when we react in ways we did not expect we would. I am not saying that there will not be occasional surprises, but at least, they will be fewer if you take time to know yourself and who you have become over the years.

An example that comes to my mind as I write this is one month where I lost my car and mobile phone within a few weeks through different incidents. I could have sat around for days complaining and feeling sorry for myself because these are things that make my life easier and more organised, but I did what needed to be done (in terms of insurance and replacements) and got on with life as normal. I had learnt years ago that I am the type of person that likes 'homeostasis' in my life. I like to have time to mentally prepare for change, or else, I like to have things nice, same and under control. Thankfully, my husband also knew and appreciated that about me, so he was supportive in helping to get things replaced quickly so I could get on with my life and work. It was a blessing to have the money to replace these items even before our insurance paid out, but I am sure that I would have found another way to handle the issues well if I did not. Realising that being without a car, for example, would have led to more anxiety around my commitments and my driving, helped me to prioritise the issue and find a solution quickly. I always say that **it is not worth letting one problem lead to another.** If I had waited around for my courtesy car (which never came!) and developed a phobia for driving after a serious car accident, I probably would not be where I am today. I am sure that someone else might have had the same situation, waited two months for a new car and got on with driving without any issues, but I knew that would not work for me. That is why we are all different and need to know ourselves so that we handle issues in a way that is best for us where possible. You do not have to do things how everyone else does them, and in the same vein, we must be careful not to judge others because they will have their own reasons for the decisions they take. A spectator might judge me as being a workaholic or wasteful spender for buying a new car, to replace mine that was a write-off, two days after a motorway car crash (which I miraculously survived without fractures), not realising that the priority was not work or money. Someone else might give mental wellbeing a lower priority than getting what they are due from the insurance company, but who are we to judge? People's experiences and values make them who they are, but that is for them to know and for us to find out.

Another example would be a man who chooses to buy cars, furniture and gadgets on credit. He explains that he likes to have things now and finds it easier to pay monthly for goods bought, than it is to save money and buy later. A spectator might feel he is living above his means and foolishly banking on money not yet earned. Another might feel that he is making the most of the lending available; while yet another might feel that this man is not disciplined with his spending. Especially in a society where many feel comfortable with debt, it is important to know what you believe on this subject, so that you are not unintentionally drawn into 'keeping up with the Jones'. The man in this scenario might get a huge inheritance and clear off his debts next week, while a copycat friend remains in debt all his life, sadly leaving nothing but debt for his family at the end of his life. If having savings and good financial standing was not important to him, then he would have lived a good fancy life, but if this man valued being able to leave an inheritance for his grandchildren, he would not have died a happy man, all because he 'went with the flow' of living permanently in debt.

Some people define themselves by what they have or appear to have, so they would do anything to keep up a wealthy appearance, even against good sense. Others do not care what people think and may actually even appear to have less than they do, because they buy only what they can comfortably afford, leaving spare cash for living. Some may prefer the 'stress' of paying monthly for a brand new car over the 'stress' of having a second-hand car. For one person, being in debt is less stressful than the perceived shame of driving a cheap car or living in a rented house. For another, financial freedom gives more satisfaction than driving a fancy car or having a house on mortgage. There is no right or wrong in many of such life's decisions, as long as you are true to yourself, and not becoming a burden to others or society due to poor financial planning.

Knowing yourself and what you want out of life helps you to endure hard times and enjoy the good times. Just as living things grow, develop and excrete waste, we should also expect our lives to become richer and fuller with less junk as the years go by. As we learn more about ourselves and others around us, we are able to keep what is helpful and get rid of the unhealthy. There is no point in holding on to the bad habits and detrimental relationships when you discover them. That would be like the body trying to hold on to urine and faeces. Constipation and urinary retention can be toxic and unpleasant! It is good to know when to let things/relationships go, so that there is room for growth and development. As much as we like things being the same and under control, we must accept that we cannot control people and certain situations. In such circumstances, I choose to change my attitude towards the people/things that will weigh me down otherwise, move on and look forward to better things ahead. You cannot force relationships to continue. Realise that you have worth and if people do not value you in their own lives, there is no need to force the relationship at that level. This does not mean creating enemies; it just means that they get moved to a lower level of intimacy. You will also be moved on to lower levels of intimacy in other people's lives from time to time, whether consciously or unconsciously. That is all part of change, which is the only constant in life.

Even with a simple thing like getting used to a new phone, I realise that I could dislike and complain about my phone for the next few months, or try to understand and get the best out of it while I have it. After all, I chose to have it. I could choose to not use a mobile phone at all, or to buy a better one. There is always a choice, so next time you complain about something or lose sleep about it, spare a moment to list your options. Is it worth losing sleep over, and what are the other options? Is it worth any sacrifices, if so what is enough and what is too much? For example, I would easily miss a few parties for the sake of my medical career, but I would not risk the health of my unborn child for medicine if I felt that a stressful, high risk job was threatening my health as a pregnant woman! There are always ways to make life more enjoyable, but it sometimes boils down to making sacrifices. You cannot attend all those parties and still have the time with your children that you spend with friends. If spending time with your children is a priority, you can always cut down on your expenses and work part-time – I did this at different points in my career when I felt my babies needed more of my time. You can also cut down on your social activities or involve your children in them, if possible. This just means that you cannot do it all, but you can definitely have it all.

Knowing myself has also helped me in juggling my business, career and family. I have taken time to understand what makes business enjoyable for me, what makes family life great and what I like about working as a doctor. I try to do my best in whatever I am doing, with the resources I have, but I also set several small targets and have big dreams with realistic expectations, so that I can achieve lots without feeling stressed and unhappy. It may take longer sometimes, but that is a sacrifice I am willing to make. Life is not a race and **I am not in competition with anyone.** Just saying this last sentence out loud is sometimes enough to relieve any stress, so that you are able to enjoy your blessings and use your time more effectively. There will be many that are worse or better off than you (however you define yourself), so it is best to just relax and enjoy the ride. Be intentional and look after yourself! It is surprising, but those that are not rushing through life, compromising their values or competing ruthlessly end up building a more fruitful and admirable life.

Personal reflections and action plan

Chapter 6

I have always liked the saying, 'Make hay while the sun shines.' Let us imagine the whole of a person's lifetime as a full day. We wake up in the morning as we rise through our early years, developing and discovering the world. The afternoon is usually when we are most awake and busy, like in our adulthood. The night comes inevitably when we have less energy, like many elderly people. Some people like to have a lie-in, but as we know, they will need to catch up on the time lost later, if they are to achieve the same as someone who did not. For example, if children do not engage with the education they receiving in their youth, they will have to spend their later years earning those qualifications when their peers are already working on greater things. While some see the afternoon as a time to get more work done before it gets dark, some like to use the afternoon for a nap. They might nap in the afternoon and stay up late to work, or the truly 'gifted sleepers' can nap in the afternoon and still enjoy a long sleep at night. In life though, the ones who waste the opportunities available to them in their youth usually have to work harder for longer into their old age, or settle for less in future.

I think people 'nap' in the most productive years of their lives due to lack of knowledge or lack of motivation. Either way, the price has to be paid when that person wakes up from their slumber and realises they have to keep working hard in their old age, or take a big step down in their standard of living. The ones who settle for less and are still not motivated to do better in their later years, even after being sluggish in midlife can be likened to someone who has an early night even after having an afternoon nap. Surely, their achievements cannot be compared to one who has had more waking hours. After all this hard work during the day, rest is well deserved. The one who rose up early and did more in the afternoon can afford to retire early or do whatever he/she pleases with the night time. This does not make him better than the one who had a lie in or nap, and decides to do their work later. The main issue here is whether they were intentional about the use of their time, whether they themselves can consider their day (life) a success and if, after all is said and done, they can look back with pride at their achievements.

As you may have guessed, I am the type that likes to rise early, get all my work done before I rest and relax. I would rather realise I have too much time to spare after achieving my goals, than find out I do not have enough time and get stressed, while achieving less. The same principle applies for a typical day, as for life in general. I like to have goals for my day, get my targets met as soon as possible, so that I can relax later or even plan for the next day. Procrastination is a habit I try to avoid. Sometimes, you just will not feel like doing anything, but for me to do what I do and be who I am, I have to let my spirit/mind rule over my body. It may not happen all the time, but my aim is for this to happen most times and hopefully all the time, as I grow older. The annoying thing about procrastination is that it feels good at the time, but usually is a bad idea with hindsight. Something will almost always happen in the time you thought you could use for that important thing, making it difficult to meet the deadline. Some people are very good at getting things done in the last minute, but personally, I would rather avoid the stress it causes.

As a mother, I have to manage my time very well because my daughter or son may need me at a time that I thought would be used for some paperwork, so I try to seize opportunities as they arise to get my work done. It is amazing how much you can do in two hours when children are asleep. It is also interesting how tempting it is to watch a movie or nap with them when it is quiet. There is nothing wrong with these things, but if I have important emails to send or documents to read, it will be silly to nap and hope that I can do it at night. I have done this at times with no problems, but sometimes, something else comes up and the time I was hoping to use in the evening is no longer available and I regret wasting that time on a movie.

Having the end in sight is a good way to draw motivation for tasks ahead. Whether it is family, business or work-related, I like to focus on my reason for doing things, rather than on the task itself. I talk with my babies while giving them a wash in the morning, seeing how this is creating memories for them and a strong bond with me. It might be easy to get a nanny or grandmother to do it, so I can do other things, but I prioritise that because I know what kind of close relationship I want to have with my children. Some 'bonding times' turn into arguments or toddler tantrums, but you have to be there for the good *and* bad times as a mum. Other mothers may bond with their children in other ways, but I find that the mornings and evenings are the best times for us on weekdays because of my work and business. Sometimes, when people ask me how I manage to do all the things I do, I find it hard to explain because it is mainly about my vision. When I put the hours in, working on my career, business or charity, I see the future I want calling me on.

It is just like working hard for an exam. The thought of results day, smiling and seeing an 'A' grade next to my name will make me work hard even when there are possible distractions. The opposite of this is the fear of failure. I do not subscribe to fear as a motivational tool. Some people work hard for fear of the shame of failure, the loss of their job or condemnation from others. I would not advise anyone to dwell on such fears no matter how likely they are to happen. **Fear cripples the mind and causes people to act irrationally.** For example, a man who fears disapproval from his boss may consider doing something against his good core values just to impress, which might end up landing him in more trouble than he feared. The man who is confident in himself, hopeful for a bright future and determined to succeed may take longer to impress the boss, but will certainly not compromise himself to achieve success. It is amazing that such a man will impress the boss and many others, without even trying, just by being a diligent and focused person.

Having the end in sight can be difficult when it seems as though no progress is being made, despite your hard work. It is important not to mess up a good trajectory to success due to impatience in tough times. If there are things that can be changed to make the journey more pleasant, by all means, do so; but please do not, for the sake of a little discomfort, lose the big prize. For example, a woman who wishes to become a company director starts out as an administrative staff in a company. She soon finds out that there is room for career progression and she can be eventually promoted to director level and possibly own that company one day. She is not that keen on starting a company from scratch, but when she imagines herself at 50, she sees herself as the boss not a junior member of staff. After two years in the company, this lady begins to get bored with the work, despite already having two promotions in two years, taking her closer to top level management. She becomes complacent with work and starts becoming obsessed with the thought of moving abroad to see if she can get a managerial post in a smaller company *right now.* She does not have money to start up her own company, but can see that the current company where she works is treating her well and she could be a director within the next four years. She is very keen for this post now because she feels that she can do the director's job already and cannot imagine working 'under people' for another four or five years. Would it be wise for this lady to leave a defined path for a director post in an established company for a promise of a higher position in a more unstable company and economy? She might feel that she is not being true to herself by staying with this company as a senior administrative staff when her real desire is to be a director, and time is flying by. In the grand scheme of things, does another four years really matter if she is only 30 years old, or is age not an issue? I will suggest, in this scenario, that she could keep the end in sight and use the time she has now to build a strong Curriculum Vitae for the director post she wants, possibly through gaining more qualifications and skills. She might choose to live her dream life now and consider resignation a better idea, but only time would tell if that was wise.

If you are truly bored of your job because you are too good at it, it means you can do it quicker and use the rest of your time more creatively. The lady in this scenario could even ask for more responsibilities at her company if she feels that her skills are being wasted. The sad thing is that most people will not consider taking on more responsibilities without more pay;

but sometimes, the experience gained by doing this will open doors for greater things – it is not always about the money. I am aware that there is no real guarantee (even in a big company) because her current employer could close down or deny her the promotion in future, but I feel that life is about taking sensible risks. If she feels strongly enough about leaving the job to start over somewhere else, then she should, but there is no reason to stay in a job with a negative, complacent attitude, because that will soon begin to show up in her work performance and possibly get her fired, which will not help her long term goal. She may be willing to go start afresh elsewhere, even if it is tougher at the start, and that is fine. The main point of this case is that we should not always run away as soon as things get uncomfortable because the grass is not always greener on the other side. On the other hand, we should also be willing to take the good with the bad when we decide to take a risk and step out for a change, because the grass may indeed be greener on the other side!

Having a vision is very important if you are to be more motivated than the average Joe. No one really wishes bad for themselves, even if they talk negatively. Most people want to be comfortable and happy, whatever that means for them. As a couple, we decided early in our marriage that we wanted to be debt-free and financially stable, as soon as possible. Coming from where we did, that was a big dream. I had so much debt and a poor credit rating as a student, due to financial difficulties and poor management of my student loans. The first step towards paying off debts for us was to take wise advice and try to live on one income as a family. We valued the freedom of being able to use my income for debt repayments, savings, projects, activities or holidays, over having expensive cars and houses that would mean we both always had to work full time to keep up with bills and repayments. I remember how surprised a relative was when she visited and found out that I was taking the bus to work. "How can a doctor like you be using public transport?!" she said. I actually did not have a driver's licence at the time, but I really did not care what anyone thought. I knew that my husband and I were earning enough to buy three cars if we wanted, but we chose to spend less and pay off debts first. No one knows how much debt or profit you are in by looking at your face, so you are free to live as you wish. For us, it was important to sort our finances out properly first, without caring if people thought we were poor or stingy. When I finally got my driver's license, we also chose to buy cheap used cars early in our marriage, so that we did not have monthly car repayments to worry about, allowing us to live comfortably on one income, as we desired. By the time our first child was born, this meant that I had the freedom to work part-time or not at all. Knowing the kind of woman I am, my husband knew I would never want to not work, but it was nice to have a choice. The vision we had encouraged us through the tough years, so that we were not moved by what fellow professionals were driving or buying. Someone else will have different values, and there is no one perfect way to do things. We just need to be intentional and true to ourselves. All I can say is that, you will definitely need six cups of coffee a day if you get a mortgage you struggle to afford without always working overtime!

I think having 'little people' watching me also helps me to live a better life. Whether we realise it or not, children learn from us. We cannot keep saying one thing and doing another. They will one day challenge us and we will have no excuses. Whether it is in the area of time management, spending money, attitude to work, healthy eating, exercise or faith, we can only teach what we know. I always had such a lovely image of how wonderful I want my children to be, but I have now realised as a parent that I need to show them what I expect of them – and it is hard! When I say that there will be no swearing in my house, I must make sure that I too do not say any of the words on the barred list when I drop a mug on my toe! This involves a lot of self-discipline, which I am still working on. When I say bedtime is 8pm for the children, I have to make sure that I am not sitting lazily on the sofa at 7.30pm and procrastinating about getting them ready for bed. Thankfully, we learnt how badly inconsistency can affect children's routine while my first child was still a baby, so now, for our own good, we usually stick to the routine so we can continue to have our nice quiet evenings!

The biggest thing I think I will need to have a discussion with my children about, though, is cake. Yes, cake. They cannot have cake every day, but Mum is allowed cake whenever she wants it because she's an addict! There, I have confessed. I may not drink coffee or tea, but cakes and chocolate are always welcome. As long as I eat my fruit and vegetables, I think I am allowed some cake. I would gladly half my main meal to make more room for dessert. The only problem is that my dream life 'perfect children' were never meant to have a sweet tooth like me, so I will either have to cut down on cakes myself or accept the fact that I am already teaching them a love of cake which was passed down from my own mother! This is now a choice I have to make with no one to blame. Maybe I will eat cake and exercise more. Interestingly, whatever I choose (cutting down or not), my children will have to make their own choices about cake and everything else in future, because we all have a choice to make about how we live our own lives, in spite of our parents' actions.

For me, 'making hay while the sun shines' is about making the most of the opportunities we have now, because they will not always be there. Whether you are twenty or seventy years old, the sun is shining now, if you are reading this book. What are the opportunities around you that you have been overlooking? What have you been putting off or wishing you could do in another life? **There's no time like now.** I am inspired by a gentleman in his seventies who attends my church. He travels around the world every year to meet Christians in other countries, as that is something he feels he should do with his life. He encourages people and makes them feel loved. He could easily have thought that it is too late for him or made other excuses, but the vision of reaching so many places before the end of his life keeps him going. Watching him also makes me think about the importance of financial freedom. The way some of us young adults manage our finances, we would not be able to 'up-and-go' anywhere after retirement because we have no plan for financial freedom that does not include the word 'lottery'!

Not everyone is cut out for business or accounting, but managing our resources well, with the end in sight, helps us to have the future we imagine. There are no guarantees in life, but if you have not done your best, you have no one to blame but yourself. Resources include time, money, relationships and talent. We may not always have as much of any of these things as we do now, so it is important to work hard and manage them well while we can, so that we can truly rest when we can't work anymore. It is always sad to see people who have ruined their relationships, wasted their talent, misused their youthful years or managed their finances poorly. It does not matter how much you had but how well you used it. Regret is a terrible thing to live with, but I think most people have a chance to make amends. The question is whether we can humble ourselves to see the change required and make it, no matter how difficult.

Personal reflections and action plan

Chapter 7

If you are still reading this book after everything I said in the first few chapters, well done. Not many people will hear things like this and keep listening. This means that you either agree with me or want to learn more. I find that most people who feel they are on the right track sometimes hate to hear what they already know, while those who are living life 'carelessly' can get upset when someone tries to reason with them. I do not claim to understand more about life than anyone else, but I think that sharing how I have lived mine so far might help someone who is not sure. I would also like to point out here that I have seen these principles work well for many and am confident that everyone can lead a happy life, whatever their circumstance, if they manage their attitude and reactions to situations well.

I shared a lot about the challenges I faced as a young woman in my first book, so I will not write much about those here. I strongly believe that those challenges have made me stronger and well-rounded as a person. I may purposely come across to some as a 'dumb blonde' or a 'workaholic boss', but you can be sure that in whichever situation I find myself, I do what I can to get the best out of it. I hate wasting time and this attribute has helped me in all aspects of my life. Sometimes, it can be seen as a weakness, which I do recognise, but I try to be aware of such situations and manage myself appropriately. For example, as someone who is not keen on the outdoors, I may find myself getting irritated at the thought of just lying around on the grass 'doing nothing'. If I am with friends that appreciate such things, I may prepare my mind by reminding myself that the time is actually being invested in my friendship with that person, rather than seeing it as time spent lying around. I sometimes even organise such outdoor activities to do with my children because I know they enjoy it. If I really have so much to do that I feel that I am not able to spend as much time sitting in the park as my friends or family would like, I may reschedule the outing for a time when I can enjoy it better, or just take something to do at the same time, if possible. Yes, you might find me knitting in the park to kill two birds with one stone!

I remember a friend visited my house and made an observation that made me laugh. She told me I had a clock in every room and seemed to be obsessed with knowing the time. My husband also comments on how I like to set alarms throughout the day, so the day does not pass me by. With so many things on my plate, which I actually enjoy doing, I could easily get carried away doing one thing and miss out on something important that needs doing today. My 'silly' daytime phone alarms help when I spend a day at home with my children, so I remember to give them meals at the right time, get some important things done during office hours and do some writing before my bedtime, for example. Bedtime is not just for children. I found that being intentional with my sleep helps me to feel well rested in the morning and have a more productive day. I think this part of me has really rubbed off on my husband because he no longer likes to stay up late to watch movies he will regret in the morning. Part of having a reasonable bedtime includes having a wind-down time in the evenings. I unfortunately still have the habit of looking at my phone in bed, but I have managed to cut out late phone calls. Some people might find the late phone calls helpful, but I have recently found talking on the phone at night tiring. I used to be able to speak with friends for two hours in the evening before bed, but I think having more to do has made me cut that out because I feel it is not the best use of my time. Someone else might use the evening phone calls for their daily catchup or 'download' like I did before marriage, but it is hard for me to do that and still have time for my family daily. I am thankful for texts and apps that allow chatting so that I am able to still keep in contact with friends during the week without expending so much energy on talking. I especially do not like receiving late evening phone calls, but I have never really had to tell anyone that directly. Most sensible people realise after a few missed calls that it is best to call me earlier in the day or at the weekend. I apologise here to any of my beloved friends who prefer to talk at night, but I am sure that they will agree that I do make contact at a more convenient time after missing any call. It can sometimes take days to find a time to talk that works for both parties, but we do eventually. I also make effort to visit people and host dinners, because I find that these are helpful for maintaining valued relationships. Since I am not a machine, I have to manage my time in a way that allows me to function well in all aspects of my life (without coffee!).

Winding down is different for everyone. Someone may find watching sport relaxing, while others may prefer to do exercise or watch a movie. My husband will gladly watch the news or a documentary after work, but I would rather watch a comedy or film that does not require much concentration. It is impossible for me to be high-functioning and 'on the ball' all the time. We all need to be aware of the fact that **we are not robots and will need to replenish our stores from time to time.** When I go around doing motivational talks for the charity, for example, I find it relaxing afterwards to just watch a 'happy movie' in silence, so I can unwind. The buzz from talking to young people and hearing about their plans for the future can give me enough energy to keep going for days non-stop, but I purposely make time to be alone, or just with close family, to reflect on my work and relax. Replenishing my stores sometimes involves reading, watching educational videos and listening to other speakers, so I do not feel drained. I also enjoy reading the Bible and listening to worship music. I have learned to never get too busy for quiet time, because it is in these quiet moments that I find solutions to big issues.

A couple that goes around advising other couples about marriage, but never spend time alone together will end up with marital problems of their own. I sometimes think of myself as being in a relationship with me. It is great to have a husband, family and friends who care, but the most important relationship in my life is the one I have with myself, and God! Have you ever had a situation where your conscience troubled you and you could not get away from it? You tried to explain away your actions, but your conscience just will not let it go? You convince yourself that you are still a good person and that person deserved the mean words you said, for example, but the issue keeps coming back to your mind, until you apologise? That's what I would call a fight between you and you! Having time alone to reflect on issues and refill your stores when you feel drained helps you to have a better relationship with yourself. That inner peace will come from having a clear conscience and no internal conflict. It is amazing the number of people that walk around pretending to be something they are not. It is not always a bad thing to pretend, but pretending for such long periods has got to be stressful. A woman who pretends to like living with her in-laws, a man who pretends to enjoy his job, a child who pretends to love a sport that mum did, will only be sitting on a time bomb which will definitely explode at some point in the future. These are not bad things, and not liking them is not bad either (because we all have different personalities), but we sometimes get ourselves entangled in a mess to please others. As much as we like to give and share, we must also realise that receiving love, understanding and compassion is part of being human. We should be able to say no, step away and recoup when we need to.

I heard a famous man saying some years ago that he gives his personal number out freely to anyone that wants it. He had no problem with having it in the phone book for everyone to access, and did not seem bothered by the thought of receiving too many calls from fans. I was quite surprised because I would never have imagined doing that. He then explained that he is not ruled by his phone and would only answer a call if he had the time. He said that if someone really needed him when he was not able to answer, they would leave a message and he would call back at a convenient time. It really made me rethink my attitude towards my phone. Many of us use mobile phones and are practically attached to them, especially if we have smart phones that receive email directly. The phone makes a beep and we jump to it faster than we would run to a crying baby! Sometimes, I wonder if it would be easier to phone/text some people than to have a face-to-face conversation with them, because they are so engrossed with their phones even when you are right in front of them! I will not deny that I have had my moments of phone addiction too, especially with my business emails coming direct to my phone at all times, but I have learned over the years that the phone can usually wait.

I do not have to answer every call straight away, I do not have to respond to every message within five minutes, and I definitely do not have to check every notification as it arrives. Thankfully, the phones are able to save the information for us for later, so we can actually choose to look at it later, or choose to be rude and reply a text while someone is talking to us. I still have to remind myself of this fact most days, especially when spending time with my family. I do not want to make people feel less important than my phone, but I must admit – phones can always provide a good excuse for getting out of boring meetings!

As a student, I remember having a voicemail recording that said 'Sorry, I cannot talk right now, but please send a text or email and I will get back to you.' It must have been in the days when I used pay-as-you-go phones and did not want to spend money listening to voicemail, or maybe I thought I might be in lectures or studying when people called. It sounded like the perfect voicemail message to me, until my father left a message that said, 'It's Daddy. Call me back; I do not want to text or email!' We laughed hard about that message for weeks and I changed the recording because I realised it might make people feel like I did not ever want to talk to them, which was definitely not what I meant. **Talking is good, but too much of anything is not good**, especially if you find that it often distracts you from doing other important things.

Our gadgets should not control us, they are meant to serve us. It is easy to spot the drug addict and alcoholic, but televisions, phones and computers can be addictive too. We need to be able to recognise when anything is getting too much of our time, so we can adjust (if necessary) and lead a balanced life. I am quite grateful for the internet, which means that I can watch any programme when I want, not when it is on TV, for example. In the same vein, socialising should make our lives better not worse. Some people have created a life where they have to leave their city to get some peace, because of unexpected visitors 'dropping by' at all times to their home. Don't get me wrong – it is nice to spend time with people, but if you are constantly distracted from other priorities because of unplanned visits, it might be worth taking some time to re-evaluate things. It is nice to have friends who can just pop over whenever they want, but if you find that your family/couple/me time is constantly being interrupted by needy friends/relatives, it might be worth checking what message you have given out about your accessibility and priorities.

I believe my home should be my haven. As they say, "an Englishman's home is his castle". I do not want to be made to feel uncomfortable or stressed in my own home. Whether it is in the name of friendship, family or work, I believe nothing should make you need to leave home to find peace. I sometimes joke about going to work to run away from my toddler at home. It is a shame that this is the reality for some. They run away from a troublesome spouse, child or relative to find peace in the office. Some have made their home a dumping ground for everyone else, so that even they themselves have to leave their own house to get away from other people's problems! No matter what the situation is, I feel we must do all we can to restore peace at home, so we have that haven for replenishing our stores daily to be able to face the world with strength. You might need to work on your marriage, train your children, stop bringing work home, set some boundaries for relatives/friends or just organise your home. **There is peace and relaxation in order.**

Whatever the issue, there will be a way to restore peace in your home, if you truly value it as your place of rest. I personally cannot function in all my capacities when all is not well at home. Whether you are single, married, a parent or not, there will be different factors that contribute to having a peaceful home for you. It is worth taking some time to reflect on that, so that you can be more able to face the world and its troubles each day. When I was single and shared a house with other girls, I found it very frustrating coming home to a dirty house. I eventually had to meet with the girls and organise a cleaning rota so that I did not have to do the cleaning all the time. This improved things a lot and I was able to enjoy coming back home again. Sometimes, the man who is working late or the woman who always wants to meet up with friends/family is running away from an unhappy home. Some couples enjoy the distraction of having guests in their home so they do not have to face the issues of their marriage or children. It is worth putting in the effort now to sort things out before they get out of hand one day. Any stress or issues that may arise from setting new boundaries and managing the atmosphere in your home can never be as bad as living like a homeless person who pays a mortgage/rent!

Create the life you want to live. Sometimes it is hard to do so, but nothing good comes easy. My husband and I love hosting people and going to parties, but we are also very aware of the need to replenish our stores and have some time alone. We manage this by having a diary, consulting each other about social commitments, being intentional about having family time and accepting that time is limited so we cannot please everyone. If you like your life now, take a moment to identify what you like about it and what needs to be maintained to protect that balance. If you are unhappy with your life, also take a moment to pinpoint what exactly you do not like about your life or home situation, and do something about it. You may need to make more friends, contact long-lost relatives, or invite more guests, if you would like a more active social life. Life is full of choices – if you shut people out, they will stay out. If you let people in, they will come in. We cannot keep blaming others for what we allow. Some people get their buzz from thinking that they are liked and can please everyone. The sad reality is that there is a day coming, if it has not yet come, when you will realise that you can not please everyone all the time, and people that like you because you do what they want will stop liking you when you don't!

Are you prepared to carry on doing what people want for the rest of your life? Are you sure they will not increase their demands later, forcing you to say "no" one day and you end up being disliked anyway? Are you willing to sacrifice your peace, time and happiness every day to meet other people's expectations? It is true that we must all make sacrifices, especially if we are to share our lives with others. I do not believe in being selfish and inconsiderate. My point is that **we must be true to ourselves, give what we can and be bold enough to state what we can't.** Whatever you enjoy doing, however you enjoy serving others, make sure that it is from your heart and not out of people-pleasing or eye-service. When you need some time off to rest and replenish your stores, enjoy that time without guilt, because those that care for you will be glad you are looking after yourself. Those that don't will only focus on what you did not do, rather than what you did for them. Be intentional about taking time out for yourself and the things that matter to you.

Even mothers (who are the greatest example of sacrificial giving for some) also need to take time out of caring for children to look after themselves. The mental health of mothers is very important and should not be taken for granted. Your children should not expect you to be a superwoman – they should understand that mum also needs rest and time for herself. Whether you have a helpful spouse, house help or none, take responsibility for your rest time, get a babysitter and take a break. Top managers and directors usually get more annual leave allowance than junior staff in companies. Whether they take it is another issue! If they can get weeks of paid leave to recoup after all their hard work, why shouldn't you take time to do so too, whatever you do? The important thing to remember, though, is that **the difference between rest and laziness is whether the relaxation is done** *before* **or** *after* **work.**

Personal reflections and action plan

Chapter 8

As a healthcare professional, I often see people with health problems. Some are sicker than they look, while others act sicker than they are. I have to say that working in healthcare has helped me to be more patient with people that magnify their problems. This is mainly from the understanding that **perspective is everything**. For one person, a cough might be a small problem ("At least, it is not cancer"), while another might consider it the worst problem in the world because he is normally very healthy. Unfortunately, there are people who have to live with long term conditions and sometimes even get defined by it. Some conditions are more obvious than others. People with depression, diabetes, hypertension or epilepsy, for example, may look completely well most days, while others get labelled as the 'autistic boy' or 'the girl with cerebral palsy', because their condition is more obvious. It does not really matter what the condition or label is, what really matters is how one sees him or herself.

Some people enjoy the sick role and enjoy being 'looked after'. They may never admit it, but they constantly expect help and pity for their condition. They are not willing to push themselves or even take responsibility for their own health, because they feel that something bad has happened to them, therefore everyone else should look after them. It is this kind of people that I have had to exercise the most patience with, because this attitude is completely opposite to my personality. The patients I admire most are the ones that take control of their circumstances to the best of their ability, learn about and manage their condition well, so that they can live a good life with as few restrictions as possible. This goes back to the point of interdependence. Those that accept the professional help available and do their best to manage their condition well usually have better outcomes than those who expect their doctor and family to do everything for them because they are 'sick'.

In most developed countries, disabled people are able to have fruitful lives if they want to, with all the support schemes and adaptations available. It is amazing though that some people have all the government funding for helpful gadgets, home adaptations, mobility and home care devices, yet they are never satisfied. They keep looking for more benefits to claim, more issues to complain about and never try to think of ways to contribute to society in spite of their disability. Then, you meet others who take all this support and achieve great things despite their challenges. Some people, even in developing countries, choose to see beyond their health problems, and make themselves useful to society despite the excuses they could have had. It seems that it does not matter what kind of funding or support people get for their condition, but what really matters is their attitude towards it. You can choose to stop working and become a liability after a small accident, or look for ways to stay active and productive despite a major injury. I know that many factors contribute to people's choices regarding working with health problems. Sometimes it is actually not possible to do a regular job with certain conditions, but this does not mean that people should consider themselves useless. Some have started businesses and support groups because of their health challenges. Many have raised funds for charities and encouraged others by sharing their stories. Others volunteer for medical research to find better treatment options for the future. Basically, they are deciding not to let the condition or illness hold them down, they are choosing to be useful to themselves and to the society, despite their circumstances.

Indecision is something I find very frustrating. For me to function as I do, I like to be able to get the available facts, make a decision when faced with one and move on. Sometimes it might be difficult to make a decision quickly as I have to wait for some vital information. At other times, I have to decide to 'wait and see', but that, too, is a decision. Sitting on the fence, especially when it is a decision that involves others, usually ends up causing problems, misunderstanding and waste of time. When I have done that in the past, I found that I ended up making a hasty stupid decision eventually. This does not mean that I always make good decisions, but I think that being decisive helps me to keep moving. I learn from my mistakes whenever I make a wrong decision and move on. As they say, "Anyone who has never fallen has never walked".

Mistakes are part of the learning and growth process. Obviously, we all hope not to make any major or expensive mistakes, but we should not live life afraid of making wrong decisions. I will actually respect someone who makes a sensible decision in a timely manner more than someone who takes forever sitting on the fence not being able to make up their mind. This does not mean that we should feel rushed with our decisions. Sometimes, the wisest thing to do will be to 'sleep on it' or 'phone a friend' and talk it through, but let that be intentional. People who avoid making decisions end up bearing the consequences of other people's decisions. They let life happen to them, rather than making things happen.

Lack of confidence (when it comes to making decisions and choices) has led to many lost opportunities for some. I remember seeing the 'perfect house' some years ago with my husband and deciding straightaway that we wanted it. Some people would advise one to go home, think about it for some time, view some more and make a decision later. This is sometimes a good idea when there is no inner conviction, but when you are sure that it is what you want, dragging your feet could easily throw you back into house-hunting for another six months because a more decisive person would have grabbed a good buy when they saw it. If, like me, you realise that 'time is money', you will not be pleased to be house-hunting for another six months, when you could have closed that chapter quickly and moved on. Sometimes, when people tell me what is stressing them out, I can see from the beginning of the story what caused it all, but it is mean to point this out to them with the benefit of hindsight. This is why I think that some lessons must be learned through experience. I am not in any way encouraging you to jump into contracts and purchases without doing your research. I would always ensure that appropriate research and checks have been done before committing my signature and/or money to a significant purchase.

It sometimes does not cost anything to make your intentions clear when you are sure about something. This could be as easy as contacting the agent or returning a form quickly while doing your research. If you later find something that you were not happy with, it would be easier to step back with a good reason, than to try and convince someone to sell to you after another has already started the process. In fact, being decisive and proactive have sometimes helped me to get better deals than the slow thinker.

Also, taking control of a situation and doing what I can, when possible, helps me to feel less vulnerable at a difficult or potentially stressful time of uncertainty. Life sometimes throws stuff at us that can keep us down if we allow it. Sometimes, it will be things that are a consequence of our previous actions or decisions. Sometimes, it just happens as part of the ups and downs of life. The sooner we realise this and stop complaining, the better we will be able to manage the bad stuff. I find it helpful to quickly analyse the situation or problem, find out what I can or cannot do about it, and get on with it. Personally, I also make sure that I have prayed for direction and help, because I believe that I can do nothing without God's help. Sometimes taking control, involves deciding not to worry about it and focussing on something else. This is where having a varied life and diary helps. If there is something potentially stressful in business that I cannot do anything about, I may decide to focus on my career or charity work while I wait it out. That way, I have not wasted weeks or months, worrying about something that would get better with time. The time some would have spent worrying about that business problem would have been used to achieve something else in another area of my life.

I remember as a young woman, when my first boyfriend and I broke up, I was naturally sad and could have allowed that to affect my studies, but I did not. I knew for a while that the relationship was not going well, and as I described earlier, I did something about it. After several attempts to improve things, I was actually ready for the relationship to end. I would have made more effort to work on it if it were a marriage, but I have learned to choose my battles. I personally do not think that a boyfriend is worth that much stress if one is not happy in the relationship. This is why it is helpful when people realise that marriage is a big commitment and should not be entered into lightly; and dating is very different from marriage. I would bend over backwards a million times over to make my marriage work because I take my vows seriously, but I do not think that a boyfriend is worth too much trouble because there are no vows to consider. The way I see it, if dating someone is causing you so much stress and unhappiness, drama or abuse, marrying such a person would be like signing up for a lifetime of relationship problems.

The aim of dating or relationships, in my opinion, is to determine if you would be suited together for marriage. Everyone has that inner need for connection, love and companionship. Sometimes we jump into marriage-mode mentally in a relationship, not realising that the other person is not taking it that seriously. Some women will even move in with a boyfriend, cook and clean, sacrifice their careers and goals, live for him for years, only to find out later that he was never interested in marriage or lifelong commitment. There is no problem if the woman never wanted that either, but most women I know do. It is never a surprise to me if the live-in relationship ends up going on for years before he even considers proposing marriage or feels forced to do so. Putting myself in the shoes of the man, I always wonder what the motivation to get married would be if I am already getting every benefit of marriage from a girlfriend – without the commitment!

The saddest scenarios in my view are when children are brought into an unstable relationship. Many would argue that marriages can end in divorce, so there is no guarantee that getting married before having children would provide a stable home. That is unfortunately true, but I still believe that marriage is a valid symbol of a stronger commitment. If he loves you that much, he would not be looking for every excuse to avoid being legally related to and responsible for you. The important thing is to marry someone who also takes marital vows as seriously as you do, because when the stormy days come, which they will, you will need strength from both sides to keep that marriage standing.

When I was reflecting on that break up, I remember my friend saying, "Never mind, what he said or wants – what do *you* want?". Talking things through with a friend helped me to sort out my feelings, and answer the very important question she asked. Sometimes we stay in situations because we are overly concerned about what the other person said or wants. The truth is, if I value myself and the time I am spending with someone, I need to be sure that this is what I want to be doing with my life. It is stupid to stay in a relationship because the person keeps saying they need you, but their actions do not add up. You need to know what you want in a relationship and go for it. If it means ending a bad relationship and being single, then do it! **It is better to be single than unhappy.**

I realised that what I wanted was a relationship where I could feel valued, loved and supported. It was becoming more difficult to feel that in a long-distance relationship, so for me, it was time to move on. I did not regret the time spent in that relationship because it was a conscious decision I made to give it a chance. Sometimes, the hard part is knowing when to change your mind or change direction. Being a decisive person can sometimes get you into the trap of wanting to hold on to things because of choices you made a while ago. Things change, people change. Feel free to change your mind when you need to. Obviously, changing your mind every few minutes would make you unreliable and fickle, but **a change of course after much thought and perseverance can sometimes be the solution to all your problems.**

In life, there is sometimes no right or wrong answer. Sometimes, we are motivated by our current feelings, circumstances and social contacts. The choices we make sometimes stem from self-preservation or gratification. People, like water, will usually choose the path of least resistance, but I have learned to also consider the future when making decisions. Considering the future sometimes means that your decision makes your life less comfortable now, and some people may even think that you are crazy or foolish. For example, a woman may refuse to date someone despite the peer pressure and apparent fun it will bring, because she can already see something about him that she cannot live with.

What is the point in starting a relationship that is bound to end in a break up? A man may refuse to invest in something immoral or illegal despite the pressure and profits promised, because he wants to leave a good legacy for his children. What is the point in having so much money with no dignity and self-respect? The Good Book says, "What will it profit a man to gain the whole world and lose his own soul?" A girl may refuse to abort a pregnancy despite the inconvenience and embarrassment she may face, because she knows that she will not be able to live with the guilt. What is the point of having a fake happy life with sleepless nights in tears? A boy may decide to save his virginity for his future wife despite the peer pressure and temptations, because he believes such intimacy should be reserved for marriage, and this is a way of honouring the love of his life. What is the point of giving all of yourself with every shallow relationship you have? For someone else, the thrill of the moment would be considered more important than the possible physical and emotional consequences of such intimacy outside marriage. If people always consider the present and future impact of their actions and lifestyle, they will be more able to live with the consequences. Also, if you have chosen one direction and found a better way, it is never too late to start afresh. Yes, there may be consequences for your former lifestyle choices, but changing for the better will build a brighter future for you. It just takes one moment of revelation to see things differently. If you did not know better, you could not have done better;

but if you know a better way and choose to go against wisdom, there will be no one to blame but yourself.

Friends and family like to influence our decisions as a way of showing their love and care, but we need to always remember that at the end of the day, we will be the ones to personally live with the consequences. It is easy to live carefree and hope for the best, but sometimes the outcome of such existence is unspeakable regret. I would rather be too careful than too careless. It is sad that some choices people make when being carefree are irreversible. A girl can easily lose her virginity at thirty if she no longer wants to save it for marriage, but she cannot undo a bad sexual experience and the scars of abandonment after losing it carelessly as a teenager. A man can easily quit his job and retire at forty if he decides he does not like working, but he will struggle hard to get a good job and start a career at forty if he chose to do no work in his youth. The smoker with lung cancer, the obese man with diabetes, the alcoholic with liver disease could sit and say all day how they enjoyed doing what they did when they did it, but I am sure that in the depth of their hearts, they sometimes wish they did things differently when experiencing the pain of the complications of these conditions that could have been avoided.

I know that bad things sometimes happen to good people with no obvious cause. Not every lung cancer patient was a smoker and not every diabetic had an unhealthy lifestyle. The 'innocent sufferer' could easily get discouraged and feel that all his efforts for a healthy lifestyle have been in vain, but I strongly believe that everything happens for a reason. If you are doing your best to be the best you can be and impact your world positively, even the bad things can produce something better than you imagined. As they say, some people make this world a better place just by being in it! When I look at how some people have managed what blows life has dealt them, I am encouraged in my journey through life. Whether it is the bereaved mother who raises awareness about the condition that killed her child, or the widow who raises four children well by herself or the sickle cell patient who does not let his condition hold him back or the self-made millionaire who gives back to the poor neighbourhood he grew up in – the world is full of people who boldly step out daily and make a difference despite their personal challenges. Deciding to be a doer rather than a spectator or critic is a good step in the right direction.

Personal reflections and action plan

Chapter 9

Have you ever met someone who always seems to be on a high? It always seems as if they have the best job, best spouse, best kids, best house, best car and best life! When you look at their life closely, theirs is not that different from yours but somehow they seem to get more satisfaction out of their life. If they are open, they will share their problems with you too, but when they do, it just seems as if they are just telling you about another challenge they are about to overcome, rather than talking about a problem that is about to finish them off. They seem to always find a way out of tough situations and somehow even get others rooting for them. Their positivity is so contagious and their enthusiasm is enviable.

In my experience, people like this are usually in one of two camps. Some are fakers who like to make everyone think that they are successful in all they do and have no problems. They will go out of their way to show off their successes and make them sound bigger than they are. They will only share their plans after they are fulfilled, to make themselves sound even more amazing and ensure that they do not have to discuss it, if it does not work. They like to know other people's plans and do a bit more than what was discussed, because they are secretly competing with their 'friends'. They enjoy keeping up a celebrity image socially even if they have to use credit cards and loans to appear successful. They like to associate mainly with people in the social category they fancy themselves in and hardly have any real friends that know their everyday situation. For people like this, life is boring without public attention. They will often go out of their way to get people talking about them – even if it means complaining about their 'haters' for sympathy, making outrageous social media comments or exaggerating their achievements. People might end up rooting for them because people like to associate with success, whether real or not.

I think the other group of people are those that actually have a good head on their shoulders. They always try to see things from a winning perspective, so it seems as if they never have problems. Even when times are tough, they talk positively, knowing that it is just a phase. They know when to share and when to listen. They share their challenges as a way of encouraging others, without sounding depressing. They are always grateful for what they have and make the most of it. You don't find them looking shabby, even in cheap clothes! They are not defined by material things, they live within their means and wear the best accessories: a smile, a good attitude and a kind heart. Their wisdom and grace makes them attractive and outstanding. They associate with the great and ordinary, without feeling the need to be fake. They are successful because they expect to be. People will root for them because their success encourages others.

It is nice to be around happy, successful people. The point here is to realise that we can manage our own mood and influence our surroundings. If you were interviewing people to work with, I bet you would take the one who was more pleasant over the grumpy one, because **personality is sometimes more important than qualifications**. It then seems like the happy person always gets what he wants and the rich get richer. Could it be that positivity attracts positivity from others too? We all need others to help us succeed – whether it is for our studies, work, business or relationships. Sometimes it is hard to care about our mood or attitude when there is so much going on, but if we make it a habit to check ourselves often, we will be more conscious of the vibe we are giving out and getting in return. This will in turn reduce the stress we feel or at least help us detect its source, so we can sort it out and lead happier lives.

You may already have gathered by now that, for me, happiness is not always about comfort. In fact, I have seen people who seem unhappy because they are too comfortable. Sounds strange, doesn't it? How would you describe the housewife who nags about being bored because she has no job to go to or bills to pay? How would you describe the man who complains about being bored in his marriage because his wife is very submissive, doting and faithful? I bet such a man would be on his toes if he sometimes had to beg for his wife's attention, and that woman would complain less if she knew what it felt like to not have enough money for the bills even after doing overtime at work! There are people who live in very difficult conditions, and suffer great discomfort, but find ways to be happy even with little. Sometimes, it is because such people probably expect less from life. They appreciate where they are compared to where they could have been. This is not to say that people should expect less so they can be happy. It is good to have great expectations as long as you are willing to work towards achieving them. Realising how far we have come in life also helps us to have a grateful attitude, but some people unfortunately use this as an excuse to be complacent and not push themselves further.

Sometimes we need to push ourselves out of our comfort zones to find the happiness we desire. The housewife described earlier could consider volunteering at her children's school or local charity shop, if she will feel more fulfilled with work. She may find it hard initially because it will involve working with people and skills she may not be used to, but overcoming such challenges can be very rewarding. The man who complains about his 'boring' marriage could consider joining a dance class and learning a new skill with his wife, or starting a new tradition with her to spice up their marriage. Unfortunately, many men with this mindset think of having an affair before they consider these simple options, which can be fun and show them another side of the wives they are taking for granted. It may be hard at first to do something you do not normally do together, but like any new habit, it will get easier with time. Be more spontaneous. Be more romantic.

Most times, the motivation we need is within us. We just need to put ourselves in the right situation and the adrenaline rush will get us through. Someone who finds his/her work boring because it is no longer challenging, will be amazed at how much energy they have inside them if they take up new roles that involve pushing themselves harder. It is obviously easier to stay where you are comfortable: same desk, same colleague, same task, same software, same issues and same solutions. The problem with this is that the boredom soon sets in and complacency begins to manifest in your attitude, which reflects in your work. I am not saying that people should change jobs every year to keep up their motivation, but there is nothing wrong with that if it is acceptable in your field and works best for your personality. Some people can happily work in the same role for 15 years, while some need change every two or three years. The quiet periods at work are sometimes a godsend when there are other bigger personal issues going on, so it is always good to think of the bigger picture before jumping out of your comfort zone after reading this. I remember being grateful for a less busy rotation in my medical career when I was pregnant with our first child. I could have done a diploma or extra shifts during that rotation if there was nothing else going on, but I chose to take it easy, so that I would not get too stressed, especially while also preparing for some professional exams. When I stopped medical work for maternity leave, I decided that I might get bored waiting around for the baby to arrive, so I spent time doing research to start an interesting new business. Business management was completely out of my comfort zone as a medical practitioner, but I found that learning something new and facing new challenges gave me much motivation to carry on. The weeks flew by and I was proud of my achievements by the end of the year.

I have always tried to make the most of my quiet seasons in life. Periods that others might consider an annoying wait, a waste of time or an unfortunate delay, have turned out to be very productive for me because I try to push myself out of my comfort zone to do things I have always wanted to do. I remember writing my first book during an unplanned year out of medical school which could have, quite justifiably, been spent feeling depressed. Life does not always happen as planned, which is why we need to be malleable, so we can seize opportunities as they arise. It may not always feel easy or comfortable, but if the end goal is what you desire, you need to **be ready to brave the pain to get the gain.**

As they say, "Do it afraid". Meaning that you should do what you need to do, in spite of the fear you feel. I know a lot of people do this every day, and if you are one of us, well done! No one can see you shaking in your boots when you submit that first proposal or attend that first meeting. All they will remember is that you did it. Some things come more naturally to some, than others, but that does not mean that we should just sit back and do only the things that feel comfortable. I cannot imagine that the prime minister was born with the ability to address the nation. He/she worked hard to get there. The brain surgeon, newscaster, police officer, high court judge and master chef were not born with their qualifications. They had to make a decision one day to step out of their comfort zone and learn a new skill or vocation. They might have always had an interest in the field or followed another person's example, but the important thing is that they did it for themselves. You will be amazed to hear that some of them may have even failed several times on their way there, but that does not make them less qualified today. They are just as qualified as the ones who excelled in every area from day one.

We must never let the fear of failure stop us from going for our goals. So what if you fail? Are you trying to impress anyone? Most people will say 'no' quickly, but on further soul searching, most of us will realise we have someone we are trying to impress. It could be our family, spouse, colleagues, friends or enemies! Children naturally want to please their parents. We want to hear "Well done!", "Good girl/boy!", "Brilliant!", so we do all we can to get that smile from them as children. As adults, we realise that we have probably now met or exceeded our parents' expectations, so we try to impress others at school or work. We realise that most parents love their children unconditionally, so we are grateful for their praise but really want the commendation of a boss, girlfriend, wife or friends. Some people become bad losers from childhood, so they either do all it takes to win or refuse to make any effort for fear of failure. Others become bad losers when they realise in adult life that there will always be someone else doing better, so they retreat into their shells and refuse to make any effort to improve themselves. Some people hide behind fake contentment or humility to cover their laziness and lack of motivation. Others carry on trying but also expend their energy bringing others down with negative words and criticism in the hope of getting ahead that way. There is obviously no need for this if people realise that life is not a competition.

We all like to be applauded. Everyone will have his or her moment as the years go by, but we must not live for the applause. If you fail, try again. If you can't, try something else. Those that love you will not love you less for failing. Those that respect you, will respect you more for not giving up. Trying to impress people that do not really care, whether they are relatives, 'friends' or enemies, is a lost battle. They will acknowledge your success if they have to, but they probably won't like you just because of it. In fact, some may hate you more for it, so you need to live for yourself and not for them. If you let their opinions hold you back from trying for fear of failure and embarrassment, you will have some of the biggest regrets at the end of your life. Some people say, "Everyone will laugh at me" I know for sure that not everyone knows you/me, and respectable people have more important things in their own lives to worry about!

I know that some people may have had bad parenting in their childhood and may not relate to having parents who cheer them on and love them unconditionally. In fact, some are still driven by the need to impress those distant and cruel parents even in their adulthood. My advice to any like this will be to not let your parents' mistakes define you. Like I always say, you cannot control other people's actions, but you can control your own reaction. As a child, you naturally wanted to please them when you did not know better. Now, as an adult who recognises the bad parenting that happened, do not continue to be bound by the need to please someone who does not really care. If they blame you for their attitude towards you, you should realise that you were the child and they were the adults. You could have been taught better by them if they were that amazing, but instead of blaming them for your issues now, you can choose to renew your mind and have a winning perspective. Do not let their opinions of you hold you back from being the best you can be. This is the same advice I would offer to anyone who has been brainwashed by a negative spouse, sibling or 'friend' into thinking that they are not good enough, and still wants to keep trying to impress them. Free your mind from that negativity and go for your goals. Step out of your comfort zone – win or lose, it is for yourself and no one else. Everyone likes to associate with success, so enjoy it when they come to celebrate, but do not be hindered or motivated by them, because people change.

Stepping out of your comfort zone also includes going out of your way to be a blessing to someone in need. People who give their time, energy and money to help others do not always do it out of the abundance they have. Sometimes, it is a real sacrifice, which may or may not be given as much appreciation as it deserves. Sometimes, I take a few minutes out of my day to talk *properly* with someone, who has no idea how much I have to do and what important matter I have given up to be able to spend time with them. Whether it is a face-to-face or telephone conversation, a medical consultation or a private conversation, it can make someone's day to be able to get things off their chest or hear that someone understands what they are going through. I have a friend who travelled around the world, after we qualified as medical doctors, volunteering in hospitals in remote villages. The poor villagers will never know the comfort she gave up to be in their village, offering her services for free. The hospitals will definitely not have been able to afford her services if she had charged them for it!

There is so much to gain from giving. When we share our time, home, life, skills, money or possessions, the joy that comes from wilful giving cannot be quantified. Notice, I say *wilful giving.* I have seen people that give or share out of compulsion. To be honest, I have done it at times, and learned that there is no blessing in it. The compulsion sometimes comes from societal expectations, cultural norms, a need to impress or peer pressure. I have had to learn to overcome these reasons for giving because I find that they only lead one into difficult situations and unnecessary problems. I give out of love and compassion, so I can be a blessing.

If you host someone in your home because of social expectations or cultural norms, where do you draw the line if they overstay their welcome or when their invasion of privacy becomes more than you can bear? If you give money to charity because of a need to impress or peer pressure, will you keep borrowing to keep it up or will you eventually face up to the fact that you cannot really afford it? There is so much joy in giving, but we must be sure that we are doing it for the right reasons, with our priorities in the right order. Not because of what people will say, or how kind we will look, or because 'we have to'. We always have a choice, and I personally believe that God will provide the right help for people through someone else if you really cannot help them yourself. I have heard of men who give their money to others when the bills in their own home have not yet been paid – all because of societal expectations and the need to impress. Surely, that cannot be right. With his wife's agreement, I feel it is okay if the family decides to forgo some luxuries (not necessities) in order to help someone in need. It will sometimes be uncomfortable and inconvenient to give or share, so we should be willing to step out of our comfort zone to be a blessing to others when we can. Such intentional and cheerful giving has priceless rewards and makes life richer.

Personal reflections and action plan

Chapter 10

People are always quick to say "Life is not a bed of roses", when advising someone going through bad times. Even if it were, roses have thorns, so there will be good times and bad times. Happy people can make the best of any situation, but sad people can make even a happy situation seem sad. People like that will always find something to complain about even when things seem good. I remember someone once saying that the bad thing about having a house with a drive is that people can tell when you are not home (by the absence of your car). I laughed so hard when my husband pointed out that not many sane people would decline a private parking space for that reason: "No, thanks, I'd rather have off-street parking!"

It takes just as much energy to find the bad in a situation, as it takes to find the good, so why don't we make more effort to find something to be grateful for no matter what we are going through? That has been one of my strongest coping strategies for getting through the challenges I faced in my student years. When I had to work to supplement the money sent to me for bills by my parents, I considered it an opportunity to gain valuable life experience before graduation. When I had to leave university for a year for financial reasons, I considered it an opportunity to explore my other talents. When my business was slow and money was tight, I considered it a time to learn more about marketing and work on other projects. There will be times when things do not go as planned, but we need to make the most of our time and stay positive. Having a strong winning attitude will enable us to boldly say "Yes" when rare opportunities arise.

I understand that I have a lot more to learn as a person and I do not know it all, but these principles have kept me going for years and helped others I have shared them with. I believe that greatness begins in the mind. If I can manage my attitude and thoughts, I can manage myself and my work better. Many people want to be the boss, but if you cannot manage your own self and emotions, how can you manage others? I cannot afford to be like a wave of the sea being tossed and turned by the wind. If I allowed every frustrating conversation, rude comment, annoying letter or poor outcome affect my mood and productivity, I would not get much done in my day. As we know, the days become weeks, the weeks become months, and the months become the years of our lives. If we are to achieve our goals and live out our purpose in the years we are given, we need to be able to resist the temptation for stagnancy and keep moving. We must master the ability to shut out that which threatens our growth and encourage things that make us flourish in the long term.

In the quest for personal development, it is easy to take on so much that we then begin to feel stressed or even trapped by our own achievements. **It is important to know when to stop,**

take a break or just say "No". When a venture is draining you more than it is adding or will add to you, it may be time to step on the brakes and reconsider. When a good thing gets in the way of something better, it is wise to take a break and prioritise. It is not always bad things that become time wasters. Even seemingly good things like exercise, food, work, reading and socialising can get too much and cause havoc in other areas of our lives. We need to be constantly looking to maintain the balance because too much of anything is not good. Most times, it is easy to decide what needs to go to the back burner if we take time out to assess what our goal or motivation is for doing what we do. If you are working all hours to buy your wife a bigger house when all she wants is family time, can you really say that you are working to make her happy? If you are stressing yourself out just to please others or appear better, it is time to learn how to say "No". It does not have to be rude or final, but your "No" needs to be taken seriously. If you do not mind stressing yourself because your actual goal is to please, then do it with a smile.

When you know your responsibilities, boundaries and possessions, you are more confident in saying "Yes" or "No" to things that can take up your time. For example, my children are *my* responsibility, so I would not have a problem in saying "No" to picking up someone else's child elsewhere if my primary responsibility is not taken care of. You sometimes hear of people getting into trouble because they could not say

"No" when things got too much for them to handle – even to the extent of neglecting their own children! There is nothing wrong with helping others. In fact, I have given and received help with childcare several times, but we must never get into the mindset of feeling that we cannot say "No" when we are genuinely unable to help after considering our own responsibilities. You may offer an explanation if you feel that it would help, but the message of "No, I can't." should not be ambiguous, leaving people disappointed when you do not show up.

Similarly, defining boundaries is very important for ourselves and others around us. If, for example, my job description clearly states that I am responsible for emptying the bins, I should realise that I am asking for a favour when I ask a colleague to help me empty the bins. It will be very stupid of me to get offended if he says "No" because we both know that it is actually *my* responsibility. He obviously knows his work boundary (job description) does not include that, and is confident enough to say "Yes" or "No". It does not matter if he has always helped to do it, it still remains his prerogative to say "Yes" or "No" to my request because he knows his work boundaries. It is also important to define boundaries in relationships and behaviour. A woman with no boundaries will be fondled carelessly by any man with no morals. A man with no boundaries will behave like a gentleman in Texas and behave like a dog in Vegas. A woman with no boundaries will speak carelessly to anyone, with no discretion. A man who does not enforce boundaries will be bullied by outsiders in his own home or business.

I have found that it definitely easier to come back to someone with a "Yes" after saying "No", than the other way round when it comes to doing favours. They are usually pleasantly surprised that you can now accommodate what they thought you could not. It also allows you enough time to really consider the commitment before you say "Yes". Obviously, in some situations, saying "No" too quickly can lose you a good deal or cause them more anxiety. The best answer I have found so far is, "I will think about it and get back to you soon". As long as you remember to get back to people with your decision in a timely manner, people will respect you for it. Some people say "I will think about it" because they find it hard to say "No", even when they obviously cannot do what is required. Others say that they will think about it because they genuinely need to check their diary etc. before committing. The worst ones are the ones that say they will "check and get back to you" to sound busy, polite or important, then never get back to you with a "Yes" or "No"!

Saying "No" is very difficult for some people, even when they know that it is not in their best interest to say "Yes". As children, we learn to say "No" to negative peer pressure and temptations for fear of punishment, but when we become adults, free from the watchful eyes of parents, we sometimes lose that ability, to our own detriment. For every phase of life, only *you* would know what you can handle, and what will be too much for you. My parents adopted a relative's one-year-old child when my brother was just a small baby. I personally do not think I would have been able to say "Yes" to that, but I am sure that my mother agreed to having a second baby because she felt capable. It would be stupid of a man to compare his wife to my mother and get upset if she said "No" to doing same because she did not feel able to care for two babies at once. I imagine that some women may say "Yes" to such a request to satisfy their husband, in-laws, community or self-righteousness, and then take it out on the child when they get too stressed. People cope with twins every day, but I strongly believe that God does not give us more than we can bear. If we get into problems because of our own choices, we have no one to blame, but ourselves. Sometimes, reversing the situation can be more difficult than it would have been to say "No" initially.

Where mistakes have already been made, we must be quick to forgive ourselves and move on. **The future is more important than the past. It is never too late to start afresh** and make the best of the time we have left. Even if the mistakes that affected us were from someone else, not our own, we do not help ourselves by holding grudges. Having a clear conscience and positive attitude helps me to achieve more every day. If I find that someone has annoyed me so badly that I am unable to function with a clear mind, I take time out to analyse the situation, figure out what went wrong and whether I need to apologise or forgive. If I need to apologise, I find a way to make amends quickly so I can have a clear conscience to carry on living the stress-free life I love. If I feel that I have been offended and need to forgive, I *choose* to forgive. I also try to find out how I let myself get that hurt and see if there are ways to prevent it from happening again. This sometimes involves adjusting my attitude and/or expectations, redefining boundaries in relationships or improving communication to avoid misunderstandings.

Self-preservation is a natural human instinct. One could easily become distant and cold to everyone in the name of self-preservation to avoid getting hurt, but the problem with this is that **the fence you build to keep hurt out will also keep love out.** We need to be able to give and receive love. There will always be the risk of getting hurt when you love, but I think it is a risk worth taking in certain relationships. Where people have shown beyond doubt that their character or personality, not just one mistake, is the reason why you keep getting hurt, then in that case, I think it is best to love them from a distance.

Biting more than you can chew can also be done emotionally, not just mentally. I think managing my emotional load, especially my emotional involvement in relationships with people, helps me to stay sane and happy. You need a good balance of 'normal' and 'crazy' people in your life. The crazy ones have the ability to drain you with their drama if you let them. This is why we need to be able to say "No" sometimes. I do not always have to listen to your various issues, bail you out or argue with you, but I would like to stay friends with you. We cannot avoid craziness in today's world, but too many unhealthy relationships and conversations can be disastrous.

I am sure that I am sometimes the 'crazy' friend in a relationship. The one who can't stop talking about her excitement about a new business venture, asking friends and family to come to one charity event or another, and talking about how much I am learning or have to learn to progress in my career. To be fair, I have considered this both ways, and will honestly not mind if a friend told me that they did not want to hear about something I am passionate about, which irritates them. I can usually tell when people are not interested in hearing about my endeavours, but when I get it wrong, I do not mind a polite hint because I would rather save my energy to talk to someone who cares. I like to think that most people I ramble on to about my work are people that care and wish me well. I can usually recognise people who do not have the same drive, or who consider me to be too ambitious, and we are normally able to just have simple small talk to maintain our friendship. We are all made different and one way is not better than another. In fact, I have periods of my life when I am less motivated than most, but the important thing for me is to keep going. It does not matter how slow you go, just keep moving so that life does not become dry and purposeless.

Like I said at the beginning of this book, it does not really matter if you like coffee or not. This is really about assessing your life and why you do the things you do. I do what works for me (and significant others) and I live with the consequences of my decisions every day. What really matters is having clear goals, knowing your purpose and living life to the full. Goals will be different for everyone, and may even be different at different stages of life, but we must always have the end in sight. **Do not just live for today or for yourself alone.** Do not live life just chasing after excitement and comfort, but also do not let other people or fear control your life. Allow yourself to be happy and to grow. Be intentional and build the life you want – for now and for tomorrow. The easy way out is not always the best way to go. Life should be an adventure – an adventure of growing, giving and building. I am grateful for all I have and I know that there is more to learn. I hope that sharing a bit of myself has helped you think more about yourself. Whether you think you have a few days or many more years to go on earth (no one really knows), please find your inner driving force and make the moments count. Coffee will run out, tea will get cold, but a determined, focussed mind always gets the job done.

Personal reflections and action plan